Heather is a successful personal trainer and yoga teacher with two young children and is married to David. She is pregnant with her third baby and since approaching 40 she has decided to write a memoir of her final pregnancy. She runs her business around the children's nursery/school hours and finds herself essentially functioning as a single parent since David is setting up a business and working more than 60 hours most weeks. Family life is non-stop and at times exhausting for Heather as she copes with pregnancy and running the house.

Dedicated to all the mothers and mothers to be – keep doing the best you can and be kind to yourself.

Heather Thomson

I Couldn't Even Look at a Cucumber!

The Secret Diary of a Pregnant Personal Trainer

Austin Macauley Publishers™
London • Cambridge • New York • Sharjah

Copyright © Heather Thomson 2023

The right of Heather Thomson to be identified as author of this work has been asserted by the author in accordance with sections 77 and 78 of the Copyright, Designs and Patents Act 1988.

All rights reserved. No part of this publication may be reproduced, stored in a retrieval system, or transmitted in any form or by any means, electronic, mechanical, photocopying, recording, or otherwise, without the prior permission of the publishers.

Any person who commits any unauthorized act in relation to this publication may be liable to criminal prosecution and civil claims for damages.

All of the events in this memoir are true to the best of author's memory. The views expressed in this memoir are solely those of the author.

A CIP catalogue record for this title is available from the British Library.

ISBN 9781528940696 (Paperback)
ISBN 9781398401419 (ePub e-book)

www.austinmacauley.com

First Published 2023
Austin Macauley Publishers Ltd®
1 Canada Square
Canary Wharf
London
E14 5AA

Prologue

The idea to write a pregnancy diary came about as I knew this would ultimately be my last time, and I wanted to remember how it all felt. Anyone who's been pregnant will know that almost immediately after the birth of your baby you forget how it felt.

This time round I had a few more challenges. Unlike my first two pregnancies, I had much less support from my husband as he worked up to 80 hours a week setting up his own business; also as a personal trainer my work is physical and I was the main carer for my other two young children (Robbie three and Jane five years old).

I thought it would be amazing to share this as a book to give other mums-to-be some comfort about pregnancy and beyond, to dispel some of the myths about what it is to be 'healthy'. This book is not going to preach to you about a healthy diet and exercise during pregnancy, but instead make you feel reassured that there is no normal way to be and that we all feel different during pregnancy… and that's ok.

Knowing how I was with my other pregnancies, I knew the optimism of wanting to be super healthy might not materialise. So, there's a lot in this diary about my eating habits and thoughts and feelings about this in my role as a PT.

So here it is, my daily account from nine weeks… the highs and lows of pregnancy, parenthood and family life.

Trimester One

Monday, 6th Feb 2012 – 9 weeks

So, this starts with me on a low already. Despite being pregnant and over the moon about that, it's the hardest part when you can't really tell people your good news and why you feel so miserable. I'm really struggling with nausea and have so little motivation to do simple things like housework, that the very thought of working is wearing me down. I know this stage will (hopefully) pass as tomorrow I am nine weeks – hooray!

Last night I was out with friends, and shared my secret with Kirsten at the end of the night… I was a bit emotional. I feel I'm not wanting to tell anyone because of my work and my sister has had a recent miscarriage. Kirsten is due her 3rd baby in three weeks' time, so the conversation was about babies most of the night. We had a really lovely time, although I'd been thinking about cancelling all week as the smell of perfume or anything strong really makes me ill. So glad I didn't cancel and managed a lovely chicken patia and some peshawari naan bread. The smell of coffee at the end of the night wasn't so good.

So, today I'm getting ready to go out and train a client and then take a yoga class. It's in a new venue so, I'm not sure how many people are going to turn up. I've just done some yoga practise this afternoon and I really feel like I'm already 15 weeks pregnant. My stomach has really grown and some of the poses are feeling uncomfortable. No way in my other pregnancies did I feel lying on my back or on my right side was a problem at this stage, but it doesn't feel right just now… Maybe I'm having twins!

Tonight I had another toastie, this time cheese and ham… I'm really struggling to drink water, and this isn't good. Someone like me normally goes to the loo every morning like clockwork and now it's sometimes days before I go! No wonder I feel tired and sluggish. Though this afternoon I forced myself to go out for a run when a client cancelled… I did four miles in 41.30 mins! I can't believe that four months ago, I ran the Loch Ness Marathon in average 8min/miles! Today's run was tough… If it wasn't for my job I think I'd want to jack it in early, like I did when pregnant with Jane, my firstborn.

Well, off I go to work.

Back from work, feel lousy, having not eaten for a while. Only two students turned up for yoga which isn't great. A packet of salt and vinegar crisps, then bed for me at 9.30pm!

Tuesday, 7th Feb

Woke up feeling a good bit better… Kids are sleeping longer till 7am, so that was a good 9 hours sleep! My husband David, on the other hand, was up and away by 5.30am again. Having bran flakes for breakfast still seems to be appealing enough, so I'm happy I can keep that going.

After the school-run, my four year old son Robbie and I went to a local coop, where I picked up EVERYTHING I fancied and managed to polish off most of it by the time it was 11am! This included a fruit corner yogurt (don't normally like these as I think they taste artificial), half a sunflower and honey baton (this is a surprise as anything healthy or brown has been a turn-off lately)… Followed by a cinnamon twirl pastry! This was greedy but my eyes and my tummy thought it would be what I needed and I enjoyed it immensely!

I did some yoga practise today while the going was good… This included doing the wheel and a headstand, first of these in a few weeks… Then about 20 minutes nap in Shavasana! I've been feeling really sad today as I know my sister is having to put her wee cat to sleep, so keep on filling up about this as she's going through one horrible thing after the other.

Thursday, 9th Feb

I woke up feeling a little sense of dread as I've got a busy afternoon and this worries me at the moment. I never worried about miscarriage in my previous two pregnancies, but I just keep hearing of others that have suffered miscarriages and with being nearly 38, I remind myself that every day I'm pregnant I'm lucky. The scan date came through today – 7th March at 2pm. I'll be about 13 weeks by then, if I've calculated it right!

I had five clients booked in until last night when one cancelled and I felt a sense of relief. I'm not doing very well in the cold these days… I suffer badly from Raynaud's disease, especially if I'm on the bike or standing in the cold coaching. I can have up to five layers of clothes on and two pairs of gloves and still not be feeling my fingers after about ten minutes of being outdoors. I keep buying new gloves, I've so many, I could sell gloves from the back of my car!

Well today went very well, a lot of clients had had good news and it was great to hear them share it. I ran with three of the clients, probably about ten miles in total today, and though it was a fairly slow pace I found myself breathless and struggling a bit with the hills… None of them know I'm pregnant and I feel quite guilty about this as I know, two have had miscarriages in this last year and are hoping to have family. I also feel bad not telling them my news as the conversation is about babies and children an awful lot. I really want to tell them when I've had my scan and my family knows first. I have this fear that if I tell someone that is on Facebook that this will accidentally get mentioned before I've told those I'm closest to.

When I got home tonight, I was starving and feeling pretty lousy and nauseous. I had toast on beans and the last scrap of cheese, then went to bed!

Friday, 10th Feb

I started the day with work and circuits at the park. I keep longing for a holiday and I know this is pretty much out of the question as we are skint while David's new business is in its first month. We knew this would be a tough year to be trying for more family and starting up such a big enterprise, but we both know the risks and agree that life is short. This will be a different chapter and I'm aware it's unlikely we'll see much of David even when the baby arrives (though he better be there for the birth!).

I keep joking with David that I think there might be two babies… He's not really getting the joke though and said he'll have to move out to his factory if that happens!

Back to this morning and work. I had one girl turn up for the antenatal yoga group – that's what I expected and I didn't want to let her down despite the church hall looking for £15 rental. Well, nobody turned up to open the hall so, she came back to my house for a one-to-one session. It's good to be getting more experience however, I felt quite unwell with the strong perfume she was wearing.

After lunch we had a lovely surprise visit from old neighbours and their seven-month-old baby. She was beautiful though she did manage to puke all down me and the smell was revolting. When she started crying Robbie started to cry! We were quite shocked at his reaction as he says he likes babies, but he really wasn't that enamoured or keen to give her a cuddle or a wave 'bye-bye'. He might well be a bit jealous of a new baby as he does love his mummy all to himself in the mornings! Well, when we were all saying goodbye, I had a total mental block and couldn't even remember their names! How embarrassing… They just laughed and said that the baby brain must still be there… David later said that would've been an opportune time to tell them our news, but I just couldn't tell them yet and also the kids were there too. I feel once I start telling one person I'll be telling everyone.

This afternoon I took the kids to my nephew's fifth birthday party. David managed to wheedle out of it with doing car things that needed doing. At the party, once again more strong perfume compounded by the smell of garlic. Man, I wish I could turn my nose off. At circuits today, I smelt a cigarette and there was no one even around! I mentioned this and one of the girls said 'Are you pregnant?' To which I said 'no'… What a little liar they're going to call me when they find out! Conversation was then onto the programme 'One Born Every Minute' – we seem to talk about this every week!

Got home from the party and David said I looked ghastly – I felt it! Today I've eaten my Ready brek for breakfast, two chicken rolls and a muller strawberry yogurt, two oranges, two hot ribenas, a bottle of diet coke (yuk!) and a tomato pasta dish for dinner, followed by an iced cinnamon twirl. I wouldn't be that impressed if this was the diet of my clients! Both pregnancies before I didn't put on much weight, in fact with Robbie I think I put on under two stone… I hope the same happens again, as I'd like to be a good role model for my post-natal clients after the birth. If I keep eating at this rate, it's just not going to happen.

I managed to fit in a half hour of yoga practise tonight before dinner… I was so hungry, but I was determined that I had to fit it in. Pleased with myself.

I better get to bed, it's 11pm and that's way too late for me at the moment, even if it is a Saturday night. David's already sleeping as he's at work all day tomorrow. Wonder what I'll do with the kids tomorrow.

Sunday, 12th Feb

Well, it's nice to wake up with nothing much to do. Kids were brilliant this morning, playing at 'beaches' and covering themselves in sudacrem and hydromol, while I went back to bed after breakfast! It's great how they play so well together and I get really excited thinking about telling them our news in a few weeks' time (fingers crossed). I didn't get up until tenam! This is a first for me and normally I feel guilty about wasting the morning and not getting on with housework; now I'm just making the most of any precious time I get to rest and make our beautiful baby.

We stayed in till after lunch and then headed out to Palacerigg Country Park which was super today. The kids loved the park and seeing the farm animals, especially the peacock that was roaming around homeless.

Despite all my rest this morning, I felt particularly lousy by afternoon. When we got back, I set the kids up in front of the telly as a treat for being so well behaved today, while I had a half an hour nap. I've struggled with eating much nourishment at all, well it feels that way, however I have managed grapes, an orange and apple so, I should be pleased about that. Overall though, same breakfast – Ready brek with soya milk and sugar, a fruit corner late morning and banana and cheese toasties with the kids at lunchtime. I hate spending time in the kitchen at the moment, every cupboard has a smell about it that I don't like. I couldn't even eat with the kids. Just to get me through preparing their dinner I had salt and malt vinegar crisps.

While they ate their dinner I was reading yesterday's paper and I thought I'd try the Sudoku. Blimey, I couldn't even do it and Jane kept saying how good her Gran is at it! I'm going to start trying to do Sudoku – I must get my brain working again!

David got in tonight about 7.30pm, a long day for him too. I did a wee half hour of yoga practise to try and make me feel better, but it is proving to be hard getting onto the mat when I feel like this. If it wasn't for my classes I think, I'd probably not be pushing myself to do this when I feel so ropey.

Well, it's bed for me now just after 10pm, after having had another bowl of Ready brek… Soon I'll be glowing like the little glowing man on the box!

Monday, 13th Feb – TEN WEEKS TODAY

Kids off to school and nursery today, so I'm making the most of the break from the school routine. Yes, I went back to bed for a wee nap after breakfast! I did a mass of ironing while the kids coloured in and made valentines cards for each other and their friends… They are so happy in each other's company and we are so lucky. I felt a bit guilty that they weren't out in the fresh air but, I needed to get on top of the ironing.

Dropped the kids off at my neighbour's, while I went to work this afternoon. I had a running client and she is one of my faster clients, so I felt I needed to let her know my news fairly soon. Managed a four-mile run and surprised myself that I felt OK, though I always feel I'll pay for it later in tiredness. My client was a bit shocked to hear my news, but I know she won't mention it to anyone.

Another client and then yoga session to finish at 7.30pm. To get me through the nausea tonight, I had some crisps and a ripple bar. Once I got home, I had more Ready brek. I really feel I'm missing out on the sitting down and having a meal, and feel the kids are too. Going to try and make lasagne tomorrow night for us all. I haven't got a Valentine's card for David yet, so hopefully this will make it up for him.

I was also hoping to see my Dad tomorrow, before the kids go back to school. When I spoke with him on phone he thought it was next week. I feel my mood is really flat at the moment and could quite happily just hibernate for the next few weeks. Not in much of an upbeat mood to teach my yoga classes or even see my friends. I hope this feeling passes soon as it's so unlike me. I'm going to bed now before 10pm… My favourite place at the moment.

Tuesday, 14th Feb

Jane up at 6.15am and I let her come in for a cuddle as David had got up at 5am to go to work. I wasn't too lazy this morning… Ended up going round the park with lots of friends and their kids on bikes at 9.30am! David had left me a lovely Valentine's card and a packet of salt and vinegar crisps! After saying last night that he hadn't got me one! So, off to the supermarket this morning to get a card and some treats in.

My notion for lunchtime was cottage cheese and prawns in a wrap. I haven't had cottage cheese in years, but it went down a treat, topped off with a 'mom' morello cherry yogurt. I had been feeling a bit better today, despite less sleep and no naps, though this was soon to catch up on me as I found out later.

Robbie had a BAD toilet accident which he's never done before, and it was a rotten smelly mess to clean up. I started to feel a bit more crabbit as the day went on… Usual things that wouldn't normally get to me. You know the small everyday things like the kids not tidying up their toys and pulling more out. Then, while I was making the dinner, Jane came into the kitchen telling me that 'Robbie has been cutting my hair!' Well, he managed to cut more than a little off each side, so my reaction was anger and rage to start with. Both were put on the naughty step and then once I had calmed down I saw the funny side of it. Robbie wouldn't eat his dinner, so was pretty much spoon fed his lasagne. They both got a little pink French fancy after dinner; my way of saying "I love you" on Valentine's day.

I was so glad to get the two of them to bed, exhausted and very tetchy and that was just me. I'd left some bleach in our bedroom sink as David had said it was mouldy. It wasn't much, just enough to cover the plughole, but Jane had put her fingers in it, when using the sink at bedtime and she was really upset about it. She thought it was my hair dye!

Ah well, once David got home we had our reheated lasagne for dinner followed by a chocolate muffin with fresh cream. I don't normally eat fresh cream as I've got a lactose intolerance, but at the moment I'm not caring. I'd also bought a bottle of shandy for us to share and this went down a treat. During my other pregnancies, I hadn't touched a drop of alcohol and I even felt guilty having a bit of shandy! Well, my philosophy is, if I fancy something, I'M HAVING IT!

Wednesday, 15th Feb

Well, back to normality with school and nursery today. Strangely, last night I was up several times with both Jane and Robbie. Robbie had wet the bed, he's never before done this, and Jane was up three times saying, it was too dark (even though the bathroom light was on). Jane confessed at breakfast time that she'd asked Robbie to cut her hair… And, of course, he'll do what his big sister asks him to do! I felt a bit sorry that she allows him to take the blame for things.

My Mum phoned after the school run and I was feeling pretty moody and grumpy this morning that I found it hard to be upbeat at all on the phone. I felt really bad about it and sent a text later saying sorry. She was trying to make arrangements to see me this Sunday for my birthday, as she goes to visit my brother in France this week.

Anyway, after the lack of sleep, I wasn't holding out much hope of having a great day on the energy level front. Well, I was pleasantly surprised. I was cycling with one client, and it was mild enough to have a thin pair of gloves on and then jogging three miles with the next client (about 12min/mile pace so totally manageable). It was a beautiful, almost Spring like day and this made me feel great. The lure of warmth was really uplifting.

A school-Mum took Jane and her girls to the hairdressers after school. She had planned to go anyway, but this was perfect timing as it meant Jane's scarecrow hair could be made into a style again! She now has a very cute, very short little bob! I think, David needs more than a little convincing that she suits it, as he said to Robbie "look what you've done to your sister's hair!"

In the evening, I had my jogging group followed by the yoga class. Again the turnout was not so great, with only nine students, however, I think I talked a few clients out of coming earlier in day! Honestly, I wonder sometimes, if I'm trying to run a business anymore! There was a new student and she was so lovely; it's this side of doing the class that I love the most. Seeing everyone at the end of the session looking happy and relaxed makes it so worthwhile.

I feel I ate pretty well today too: quite a lot of variety including a roasted pepper stuffed with cous cous, mozzarella and balsamic vinegar. After yoga, I had a prawn noodles dish which David had made, but this was a bit too spicy. I enjoyed this while watching my weekly favourite 'One Born Every Minute'. The show tonight featured a midwife who went from hoping for a natural water birth to having an epidural and a twin delivery. Well, you can imagine the twin delivery had me sobbing my heart out… I really do wonder if I might have twins!

Thursday, 16th Feb

Today has felt like a slog… I seem to have one good day followed by a harder day the next day. David has been in England today, so he leaves early and gets back late… Nearly 9pm and he's still not home. After the school run, I took Robbie to the gymnastics parent and toddler session. His friends Blake and Kieran were also there, so they all had a great time. I felt so sick despite all my breakfast, so had toast and crisps as soon as I got back after 11am. Eating a lot of crisps doesn't fill me with joy. I'm trying to drink as much water as possible, but have only managed two glasses today, which I downed in one to get it over with. I had scrambled eggs on toast for lunch which was brilliant. I could've eaten it all over again!

Once I'd dropped Robbie off at nursery, I tried to get some of my antenatal yoga posters put up in clinics where antenatal classes are held. I had no luck as I'd need to be taking the class there, which is fair enough. I then came home and decided my bed was the only place for me for an hour. When my alarm went off, I felt worse than before and really didn't want to move an inch. I had another ten minutes and then got myself in gear to collect the girls. On one hand, I feel disappointed that I'm not keeping more active or doing yoga and on the other hand, I just think that this rest is needed to make a healthy baby.

Tonight Jane had a school Valentine's disco – I picked up all the girls with Robbie to take to the party. Jane's friend had some of her Mum's perfume on, so I drove with the window part down as I thought I might vomit. I'm feeling really rotten and nauseous today.

I made tuna pasta with mayonnaise for my dinner and ate two big bowls full. Just about to watch another programme about birth and Dads called 'A Dad is Born' – I'm obsessed! Good night!

Friday, 17th Feb

Another day where work is mostly in the evening, when I least feel like working. Robbie was brilliant this morning and I managed to motivate myself to get tidying up and hoovering the house, while he coloured in for several hours. I dropped him off at nursery and trained my first client at the park. We did a few miles running which felt fine, in fact, I didn't feel as breathless as I have over the last few weeks.

I had a gap in the afternoon which I used to practise yoga, have a 20 minute nap, do some research for my antenatal yoga class and then have a shower. I felt guilty that I didn't pick up Jane earlier from a neighbour's, however I feel I shouldn't have to justify that just because I'm at home, doesn't mean I'm not working.

Later tonight, I had two more clients both out running, so in total today I probably did eight miles of jogging, though not at a fast pace. I ended up telling my last client about my pregnancy. I felt I had to as every session she has, she brings the subject to having children. She asked "if I were to fall pregnant in 6 months' time can I still exercise and run?" It turns out she is desperate to start a family. I totally understand where she is coming from, as even though I have two healthy children, I longed for another for about a year. David would joke and laugh off ever having a third baby. It really started to consume me and I could think and talk of nothing else. Eventually I had to be honest with myself, and have a chat with David about it. I think, doing my yoga teacher training gave me the strength to bring it up.

I had been so surprised at David's response not being an outright 'no' that I burst into tears. David had said he would sleep on it and that was good enough for me. In the morning he had asked if I needed anything else from the supermarket and I suggested 'folic acid'! Well, when he brought home folic acid that was me, I couldn't stop smiling.

Back from work and David headed back out to work… It's a good job, I fell pregnant quickly as his time in the last two months has been completely taken over with setting up the new business.

Saturday, 18th Feb

Well, this Saturday started differently… Normally, I have an outdoor circuits session at 8.30am, but yesterday I decided I needed a morning off this routine, especially with working the Friday nights till 8.30pm. I later regretted this decision as it is my business and a loss of at least £28 for an hour of work. I kept the antenatal yoga class as I'm still trying to build this up… Only two pregnant ladies came. Unless I get more, this isn't going to be sustainable.

I went a brisk 30 minute walk at the park, after yoga to get some fresh air and see if it would make me feel better. I knew the rest of the family would still be out so, I had nothing to feel bad about. By the time I got home, I felt so nauseous, it was rotten. David got back with the shopping and I immediately ate a strawberry fruit corner which made me feel human again. So much so that his joke about buying me a packet of sweets called 'sour faces' made me laugh! We all had a lovely family lunch together. I ate three separate instalments of baguette and roast chicken washed down with Irn Bru. This really disappoints me as I haven't touched sugary fizzy drinks in years, let alone to be drinking them now while I'm pregnant. Really suffering from a sluggish bowel though and lack of fluids is the main reason.

Later, we all went a walk up the street and bumped into a neighbour I hadn't seen in a long time. It turns out she is expecting again, twins in July! So this is great news… She already has a little girl who will be two when the babies arrive. It's great to hear that someone else is expecting around the same time as me. She's 16 weeks at the moment and hopes to come along to some of the antenatal yoga classes.

Tonight we had a supermarket 'Indian takeaway'. I had the chicken korma and rice. Even writing this just now could make me feel like barfing, it really didn't agree much with me. David and I watched a film 'The Ghost' with Ewan MacGregor and it was great! Really nice to spend some time in the same room together!

Sunday, 19th Feb

Ah Sundays, a day for a long lie in while the kids play in their bedroom. David had left for work by 6.30am and the kids were up just after then. We all had breakfast and then I got back under the covers, napping and watching the news till about 8.30am. I felt a bit crabbit this morning and there was no reason other than these raging hormones. The kids played great, even if they did turn their bedroom upside down!

My breakfast today was crunchy nut cornflakes and all bran – this used to be a favourite of mine when I was a teenager!! Full of sugar but hoping the roughage will help me go to the loo! Then by the time I got up, I was feeling sick again and had a fruit corner. I managed to squeeze in a half hour of yoga although this was gate-crashed by the kids… And rightly so, as I hadn't spent any real time with them this morning up till then.

We headed to meet my mum in Glasgow. This was to be my birthday treat as she is going away this week to visit my brother and family in France on Wednesday. I had a baked potato with egg mayonnaise – it wasn't even on the menu but this is what I'd got my heart set on. Jane ate tonnes and we all even had a dessert. I can't remember the last time I've had a dessert when I've been out for meal, but the apple crumble and custard went down well. Jane had profiteroles and ice-cream and Robbie had ice-cream. We all then went to Kelvingrove Park for a walk and the kids were on their bikes. Then we ended up back at Mum's. I hadn't planned for this however, it was really nice. Mum even let me have a sleep – she thought I looked really tired so, I said wake me after 20 minutes, well I think she let me have a good 45 minutes!

I ate again, this time a cheese sandwich and then we headed off home just after 6pm. The kids were sleeping within about ten minutes so, it was a quiet journey home. When I lifted them upstairs to bed I couldn't believe the state of their bedroom… Not a cover or a mattress on their beds! So, I eventually got them into their beds with them barely waking up… So now I've broken one of my golden rules to always brush their teeth! I had to eat again as the nausea just keeps on rising – this time two packets of salt and vinegar squares crisps!

Well, now I'm propped up in bed and it's nearly 9pm and David still isn't home. I'm really worried he's working too hard.

Monday, 20th Feb

The kids were up bright and early at 6am, no surprise really after their early night last night! They decided to play 'aeroplanes' out on the landing – piling up their mattresses again and mimicking all the noises a jet plane would make. It was hilarious.

After dropping off Jane at school Robbie had a breakdown in the car, sobbing his little heart out as I drove past the street that would take him to nursery. He said it was a 'Jackie' (his teacher) day and he wanted to go to nursery all day! Nothing like feeling loved. Decided I must spend a bit more time with him in the mornings, as often he is so well behaved he seems content enough to play on his own. So, we read books for about 30 minutes and then I got so sleepy, I felt my eyelids were closing. Robbie went off to play with a suitcase for a while and I had a wee 15-minute lie down on the couch.

After dropping Robbie off at nursery, I had only one client as another had cancelled last night. We were outside running for about 3.5 miles and at a gentle 12.5 minute mile pace. The weather was pretty wild and wet but refreshing. I feel like I've done nothing but eat all day. Chicken sandwiches, cheese and banana toasty, crisps, Ready brek. The nausea seems to be getting worse and my mood is very low. I had another outdoor session early evening – I was freezing but glad it was conditioning work and not running intervals, as I've not told this client about my current state. I know how much she wants to fall pregnant and I feel bad not telling her but also think she would mention this to other friends she has that are on Facebook.

Since coming home, I've felt more nauseous and tired than ever. I'm really struggling with this and pray that it gets better next week. I have a feeling already that this baby will be a little girl, as with all these hormones it's got to be!

Tuesday, 21st Feb

Woke up with a good feeling, as today I had no work on in the afternoon and was looking forward to just going with the flow. My friend came around this morning with her three year old daughter. We hadn't seen them since before Christmas so, it was great to catch up and share our news. Robbie and Kate had a right good giggle, especially the moment one of them launched Jane's wooden baby cradle all the way down the stairs! It must be made of strong stuff as it didn't even break. I felt bad as I gave them both a little telling off, nothing compared to what I'd have done if it had been Jane and Robbie, however Kate burst into tears. I felt like such a baddie!

My neighbour then popped round too with some banana loaf, which was delicious. In return she got my 'hypnobirthing' book to read. She's due to go in for a third C-section in a week and is having serious thoughts about trying to go naturally herself.

While I had a few hours to myself this afternoon, I popped over to the shops and bought my sister a birthday card and present. Came back home and had a 20-minute sleep. I've got to fit them in!

I picked Jane up from school and she was in a rotten mood. She said she was hungry despite having a hotdog and pancakes for 'American Theme Day' at school. The mood got even worse, when we attempted homework and I found it hard to conceal my disappointment that she had so much work brought home unfinished from during the day too. It wasn't a good start. Jane seems really easily distracted and her writing and work at school looks quite poor in comparison to what she can do at home. I decided to write something, along those lines, in her homework book for the teacher to see.

We all had a baked potato and cheese and beans for tea. I've eaten a whole tub of cottage cheese today, I just couldn't get enough of it. After bedtime, I phoned my brother to catch up and tell him our news. He was delighted but very shocked. I hope to see my dad tomorrow and tell him the news too, then it'll be just my sister I need to tell and I'm really not looking forward to that.

Wednesday, 22nd Feb

My dad sent a text first thing this morning saying he couldn't make it today. I felt disappointed and then thought I'd get on and make plans with Robbie. We went swimming this morning and had such a brilliant time. He giggled and charmed the lifeguards and swam his little socks off. Such fun and great company. On the way back home, we stopped off at the shop again today for two tubs of cottage cheese.

I've felt so much better today and not been as nauseous at all. Please let this be a breakthrough and keep going. I've kept thinking about getting out a run this afternoon, despite the weather being windy and wet, so I am on a roll today. My run today might have been a slow 4.2 miles, but that doesn't bother me. I just enjoyed being out in the fresh air and running at my pace.

I picked up Jane from school and we had a nice time just mum and daughter, though mostly spent doing homework. More uncompleted work sent home. It's not right, a five-year-old spending an hour on homework! I feel rotten for her, but I also don't want her to get behind with her work. She did really well though and right after it she started tidying up Robbie's mess! She did say she was trying to be good all day, and this morning when she'd got up, she said she wasn't going to be grumpy after school today. I asked her if this was hard work and she said 'yes'. So funny.

Well out to work tonight, a good jogging session followed by my yoga class. A better turnout of 13 students so, I'm delighted with that.

Came home and within five minutes David had left for work again. I sat and watched 'One Born Every Minute', my Wednesday night fixture. I pretty much cried all the way through it and find it so hard to watch when we see things going wrong. I just hope all goes well with my pregnancy and that the scan shows everything is OK. Two weeks today and we'll hopefully know for sure.

Friday, 24th Feb

Well, I didn't write my little 'diary' yesterday. I thought I'd have a day off, and anyhow it was mostly nausea and eating dairy foods! Though I did make myself go for a swim in the afternoon which made me feel a bit better.

Today has been a good bright, though windy day. Went a walk with my neighbour and our boys on the scooter this morning and I was freezing. She is booked in for a C-section next Wednesday, though is desperate to try and have a natural birth. If she starts naturally they will allow her to progress, otherwise it's the section.

So, she's on a mission to eat as many curries, pineapples and as much raspberry tea as she can manage over the next few days!

I was on my bike for two hours this afternoon with clients. I really enjoyed it. I also managed to clean my groundsheets for circuits training tomorrow morning so, I've had loads of fresh air. Last client tonight was also outdoors in the clients back garden. She gave me a beautiful big surprise bouquet of flowers for my birthday and to say thank-you. I was overwhelmed, it's so nice to be thanked and given a surprise. I got home earlier than my normal Friday times, as two clients had nights out arranged. This was good as I got to see everyone and sit and have a proper dinner all together as a family.

Today I've eaten a shed load of cheese, cottage cheese and yogurts – I really don't like eating this amount of food and hope I stop eating so much soon, or I really will put on the pounds this time round. My body must be craving calcium, fat and protein big style.

Well, I'm knackered now, David is back at work tonight and I'm in bed and planning on sleeping very soon. I must've turned a wee corner this week though, as I haven't had a nap during the day for several days now.

Saturday, 25th Feb

My birthday! Woke up to the kids singing me Happy Birthday and giving me my present… A silver ring with an opal stone from Ortak, chosen by me. I then got up to get ready for my circuits class and antenatal yoga class. David must have had about five hours' sleep so, was having real difficulty waking up to get ready for taking kids to Jane's gymnastics.

We had a bit of a tiff this morning (I was feeling a bit crabbit), as David asked me what I'd like to do for dinner for my birthday. He'd tried loads of places yesterday for us to try and get a stay over in a hotel with spa facilities, but to no avail. I just wanted to be out of the house as it constantly reminds me that there is loads of housework to do. The kids were going to have a sleepover at their Gran and Pappy's so, I wanted to make the most of it.

On way back from work, David called from the supermarket saying they had no 'normal' cottage cheese, just 'low fat' stuff! Am I really that difficult… Ahem yes at the moment!

David arrived back with the kids just as our neighbours had popped in with a delicious iced ginger cake for my birthday. Robbie was whispering that they had also got a cake for mummy and it's a secret. Aw, he is so cute it's unbelievable.

We all had our lunch together. I had a couple of chicken rolls, a bagel and then some of each of the cakes! I am eating a bit much.

Managed to get a last minute facial and haircut – this was fab, I really was getting fed up looking at my long dreary locks! So, now I've got a shoulder length bob which I really like. By the time I got home, David was taking the kids to his parents.

A quick change and then David and I headed into town to 'Gandolfi Fish' restaurant. I'd said to David I'd like something a bit healthier like seabass with vegetables, so David had booked here. Well, it turned out there was no seabass on tonight and most of the menu was off the cards, because of shellfish and their homemade mayonnaise having raw eggs in it! Well David enjoyed his and I ate tonnes of bread and a white fish, can't remember what it was called with a buttery mash. Lots of David's chips too.

Then to the pictures and a bucket load of popcorn and coke. There ends a good birthday with way too much food!

Sunday, 26th Feb

Well, David and I slept till about 8am! I think (I know!) he was looking for some nookie, but I'm just not interested at the moment and would rather wait till after the scan too. So instead we went out on our bikes for 45 minutes. We never get the chance to do any exercise together and we both love going on the bikes. I'd felt my throat a bit sore this morning, when I got up and on the bike my head was so cold. I really hope I don't get a cold now.

David left for work right after his shower saying he would see me tomorrow, it was going to be a long day! My mum-in-law took the kids to mass and brought them home about 11am. They'd had a great wee sleepover, but a late night and were pretty tired. We didn't do much today, in fact Jane and I had a cat nap on the sofa under a blanket. Lots of colouring in, painting and reading books followed by dressing up and tidying up. A roast chicken dinner went down well and David even came home for a plate, when he heard there was one made up for him.

Off to bed now at 9pm. I've a busy day ahead with five clients from 1pm till 8pm; all outdoors and lots of running. I'm going to be knackered.

Monday, 27th Feb

I had big doubts about getting through today and now I'm sitting here. I'm relieved, it's over and I managed it. The weather stayed kind to me as the forecast of heavy rain didn't happen! I woke up feeling extremely nauseous. I'd been up a few times during the night with Robbie and David getting in from work at 2am (I'd left my key in the door and so had to go and open the door for him), so don't think this all helped.

I did an ironing this morning after playing with Robbie... He was happy, sticking and cutting and making a general mess. Then I had a lie down for 30 minutes, while Robbie watched telly. I really felt I needed something to get me through the day.

All sessions went well, without overdoing it on the running stakes and without having to tell anyone that I am pregnant. I was so hungry by the time I finished tonight, I thought I'd be sick. Today I ate Ready brek and all bran at breakfast. Then needed a fruit corner after dropping off Jane at school to take away the nausea (it didn't really work). Lunchtime at 11.30 – two wraps and cottage cheese and chicken – didn't even enjoy this. That lasted me till I had a snack of a banana and cereal bar later in day between driving to different clients. Dinner tonight, on text request, was a 3 egg omelette and new potatoes and salad cream…Nothing has tasted so good! I ate a kit-kat too, but this was only because I saw David had left a kit kat wrapper lying out.

David left for work after making my dinner… I've written up my work notes, done the dishes and put on a washing. Time for bed and to read up on yoga. I really wish I could fit in more practise, but I just wasn't feeling up to it this morning. I will design a new session to practise tomorrow for Wednesday night's class.

Tuesday, 28th Feb

12 weeks today…So all the organs are formed and our baby just needs to grow now, amazing. Saw my expectant neighbour at school run today… Feeling quite emotional just thinking about her going in for her C-section tomorrow morning. She said she's crying loads.

Took Robbie swimming this morning, so this was good fun and then straight to co-op to get cottage cheese and fruit corners… Bet I never eat them again after this pregnancy. Managed to reverse into a wall when I took a wrong turn; a rotten elderly man at the bus stop shook his head profusely as if to say I shouldn't be allowed on the road. GGGGRRRRR.

Robbie's nursery were having an 'Eco-day'; we were to take recycled packaging to make something together and also some toys he didn't want anymore to swap with someone else. Well, we made a rocket and then when I was trying to leave, he threw a big hissy fit and didn't want me to go. I was so taken aback and just felt like crying. (OK I did cry on way home). The nursery teacher had to actually prise him away from me, screaming.

When I got home I tried to do some yoga and just felt I had no spirit in me and no energy to give, so did some meditation with a candle and 15 minutes of yoga movement then ten minutes of Shavasana. I don't really feel it's enough for being a teacher, but it's the most I can manage.

Once I'd picked up Jane we were back at Robbie's nursery and making more things out of boxes and tinfoil. They both got a little 'tattoo' on their hands and a fairy cake. Jane did her homework brilliantly tonight and they both ate really well at dinner time. Just as well as I've had no energy left to argue.

Jane came out with a cracker at teatime tonight. 'Mummy how sore was it when I came out your tummy?!' My reply after initial shock was 'just a little bit sore'. She then told me that her friend had asked her mummy the same question and the mum had said it wasn't sore at all! Oh dear! Well, I told Jane I didn't want to lie to her that it was a little bit sore… Jane's labour really was murder in fact!

Wednesday, 29th Feb

Well, today has been an emotional day. My neighbours had their 3rd baby this morning by C-section. I've been welling up all day thinking about it… Could hardly even get the words out to tell Robbie, and, well, he wasn't bothered anyway!

After the school run, I went to the park with the kids and my friend. We had a good chat about it all and I felt good for having spoken a bit more about it. I really just want the scan day to be here, as only then will it feel like it's definitely happening and something to share with everyone.

My mum came back from France today, but I didn't get the chance to speak as busy with work and kids.

Jane had a mother of all tantrums tonight over 'doing her homework', 'not doing her homework', 'being too tired' and 'being too hungry!' It got totally out of control and she got herself so worked up, it was hard for her to calm herself back down to eat her dinner. David well and truly gave her a telling off which exacerbated the situation for a while. I then went off to work with my jogging group and yoga. These went well with 13 students at yoga.

When I came home, David had left me the remains of a chicken noodle stir-fry; it was delicious. I then proceeded to eat two packets of salt and vinegar crisps.

Thursday, 1st March

Today has been another very emotional day. I had a good catch up with my mum this morning and she thought it would be best if she spoke with my sister herself about our pregnancy. She did this and said it was as expected, and I've felt emotional all day since. In fact, my stomach has been cramping a lot this afternoon and it's been getting me worried.

This morning I went out to the shops with Robbie to buy some baby gifts for the new baby. Robbie seems to have transformed this week into a different boy, and not for the better! He is challenging me and wanting his own way with everything. He had two tantrums in the space of 15 minutes at the shops over presents to buy for the baby and they were full blown 'I'm going to shout this shop down' level! I dealt with it really calmly though, as much as I'm shocked he's behaving in this way. I really hope they don't last long!

I had one client today while Robbie was at nursery. It was good to be on my bike on such a lovely day.

After school home time, the only mishap was when a bowl of blueberries got mysteriously knocked over and the blueberries tramped into the carpet. I wasn't impressed as they were blaming each other. Also my patience with loud noise and children were quite low this afternoon… A combination of nausea and tiredness.

I had some macaroni cheese and baked potato and cheese for a quick dinner tonight. As David put it, that's a bit of a carbs overload! Whatever makes me feel a bit better.

My friend picked me up before 7pm to visit our friend and the new baby in hospital. She is gorgeous and with lots of fluffy soft hair. I thought being in the hospital would have made me nervous but instead it made me really excited about being pregnant and having a baby again. I ended up telling my friend my news on the way home. She was super shocked, though did say she thought my boobs were looking much bigger! Well, tonight I've been getting quite a bit of tightenings and I feel like my stomach has doubled in size.

My sister sent me several lovely texts tonight which must be hard to do. I've been more than a bit overwhelmed and crying a lot, as I really didn't expect to hear from her at all. She's been so understanding but deep down she must be thinking, *When is this nightmare going to end?* They are in my prayers every night and I really pray that life picks up fast for them.

I'm going to sleep now even though there is an ironing to be done, dishes in the sink and untidy rooms everywhere I look.

Friday, 2nd March

A fairly normal and contented day has been had… Which I feel I was due. Up a few times during the night, doing the longest pees ever during the night despite not drinking enough! Robbie and I went to the park this morning for our daily dose of fresh air. Then back home and preparing for work. Not a busy day as one client cancelled later this afternoon. Only a weights session early afternoon at park and a yoga/weights session in a client's home later.

I picked Jane and her friend up from school and then went to Decathlon for new weights – I bought a set weighing 20Kg which felt fairly heavy to carry in one hand! I was extra careful with how I lifted it though!

On my way back from my last client, I kept seeing takeaways selling noodles dinners! I was starving. My lunch of three pieces of cheese and toast and a sweet pancake with cottage cheese had been six hours earlier. Though my guts haven't been good these last few days it's maybe because of the amount of cheese I'm eating… I think it's disgusting, but it's just what my body wants at the moment.

David went back out to get some noodles – tasted pretty satisfying however left me burping the rest of the night. I'm definitely getting a little belly, even with my stomach pulled in I can see the outline of where I've grown. I think I might become some size this pregnancy. Will start to weigh myself every Tuesday I think, out of curiosity more than anything else. I didn't know my weight at all when carrying Jane. With Robbie, I went from about eight stone to 9 stone 10lbs thereabouts. This time, I started about eight stone 2lbs and am now at about eight stone four or five lbs.

Saturday, 3rd March

A usual Saturday start with circuits and even though there were only 2 clients, it was a great wee session and they loved it! My antenatal yoga class doubled in number today… to 4 expectant mums! Still, we're getting there and I feel positive about it.

Had a lovely time with the family today… usual Saturday lunch after David's big supermarket shop and too many over-indulgent goodies. We all went out to the shops to get Jane some waterproof bed sheets as she still hasn't cracked the whole night-time wetting. Really think she shouldn't be wearing a bedtime nappy at five years old. Robbie hasn't worn one since the week he was toilet trained and that was over a year ago.

When we got back, we had a surprise visit from my sister and mum-in-law. I don't know what happened with the kids, but they went hyper. We told David's sister our news and she was really happy, though pretty shocked! Although she did make a comment that she thought my face was looking a bit fuller! This has got me a bit concerned as I know I'm eating a hell of a lot more but I never thought it was noticeable on my face. Yes, my chest and tum but not anywhere else! David said he disagreed and mum-in-law said that she thought opposite last weekend when she saw me. She said she thought I was very thin and must be mistaken about pregnancy! Ah well! I didn't realise quite how in this pregnancy my appearance and weight makes more of a difference than my other two pregnancies – purely because I'm now doing a job where I'm a role model for health and wellness and as I didn't put on much weight the previous two times, I wouldn't this time! We'll have to wait and see.

On that note, we had a lovely dinner of steak, wedges and peas with a creamy sauce (David's speciality) and it was delicious. I managed to resist the chocolate fresh cream choux bun David had bought, although I had eaten a fair amount of chocolate buttons earlier in the day!

Sunday, 4th March

I had to lie in bed a bit longer and have a good think about what day it was this morning. When I remembered it was Sunday and that my dad was visiting, (maybe the first visit this year) I was very happy. (David working all day of course.)

I dyed my hair, though I'm not sure if I'm meant to be doing this or not and tidied the house. Kids were well behaved despite their efforts to thwart my tidying up mission!

It was a lovely day so we all went out to Drumpellier park with the kids' bikes.

My dad was delighted when I told him our news, I'm sure it will sink in later on with him. I also saw our neighbours with the new baby; apparently she was awake from 10.30pm–5am last night and that tonight, mum and dad will be in separate rooms! Told David later and he just laughed and agreed it would be same here!

Managed to do a good little session of yoga and relaxation tonight – broken up in about three parts, what with putting the kids to bed, but I did it all the same!

Can't believe it's only days away now that we get our scan… I hope and pray everything is OK.

Monday, 5th March

I'm writing this on Tuesday night and am trying to remember what kind of day I had yesterday! Maybe this is just a reflection of how eventful today has been… and not all in a good way!

What I remember was, it was a beautiful day and I went for a lovely jog at park. I did a mile walking, as I felt pretty tired and didn't feel like my body wanted to run. I went on to do four miles jogging and each mile got a little quicker, last one in under 9.30min/mile. I had a client after this and then a break till much later as another client cancelled less than an hour before the session.

My last session was a new couple doing yoga in their home. They were so lovely and really enjoyed the session… I felt bad that I didn't mention my pregnancy however I wanted to wait till after scan, and also I do need to try and keep my business running. Think my tummy is showing a bit though and maybe this isn't what they'd quite expect of a personal trainer! Got home at 10.15pm and feeling knackered.

Tuesday, 6th March

Well, I'm officially into the second trimester as I'm 13 weeks today… unless the scan tells me different! I woke up feeling good despite a few interruptions to my night's sleep – pee pit stops and Robbie was up for a cuddle.

I read to David my 13 week update from Netmums and he said, 'Hooray, we've made it, so that's you past the grumpy stage!' Cheeky devil. I clearly was in a good mood as I laughed. Also weighed myself today as I'm going to do this weekly on a Tuesday… eight stone three(ish) lbs – quite surprised as I do feel like I'm eating an awful lot and have a bit of a tummy!

Well, as I said, the day started well. I then went to the bank and ASDA with Robbie and he had a tantrum that lasted all round the shop… the looks I was getting. All over my choice of trolley and his mind changing three times about going in a trolley, sigh. Well, I took it all in my stride and it didn't put me off my good mood.

I had a client in between nursery and school runs and I told her my news as I'd rather tell clients in person now and the scan is only a day away. She was very happy for us and it was good to give her some good news as she's really having a troubled time with her mum suffering from cancer. We did a good four mile jog so I was very impressed with my client as she's stepping it up again.

Well, I did say my day was to change and it did seem to change when I picked Jane up from school. This morning, I had phoned the school about Jane's claim last night that she had been sick at school yesterday. She was in good spirits, had looked fine and ate her dinner fine. I always feel you have to trust what the kids are saying, even though it seemed strange she hadn't been sent home. She said she'd been sick on her pinafore but the ladies had cleaned it up with a baby wipe. She also said she was lucky she hadn't been wearing her watch as this would have got ruined.

Well, when I spoke to the school it transpires, that a number of children had claimed they felt sick. They had a different teacher yesterday afternoon and it looks like a few of them thought they could play this game. I'm more annoyed with Jane that she can fabricate the story and even more last night about the details… which never happened! Jane even denied it again when I asked her for the truth after school. Then she asked, 'How do you know?' And I told her I'd spoken to the school. I told her off and said she'd get no telly tonight and that was it over with. On the way home in the car, Jane started telling another story about not getting her playtime or PE today because she was too slow at finishing her letters. I was really angry that she would be denied these breaks and time to exercise that I was going to phone the school as soon as I got in. Then Jane said, 'I'm just kidding!' Well, I snapped, driving the car, and screamed at her for lying again after just being warned that lying was going to get her in more trouble.

I sent Jane to her room and have found it very difficult to snap out of this the rest of the day. Anything she objected to with her homework made me snap and I felt like Cruella de Vil by the time they went to bed. There have been too many tears from everyone today. I'm exhausted and after putting the kids to bed I've been in mine, doing some work. Feel like a rotten mum, and the day had started so well.

Wednesday, 7th March

Well, today is the day. We get our scan this afternoon and I'm feeling more than a little on edge and scared. Today, I made all the effort I could to drink lots so that I'd have a full bladder for the scan. I remember doing that with Jane's scan and totally forgot with Robbie; it really made a difference.

I went to the park with Robbie in the morning and his bike. Our first attempt, to get out the door was dashed as the hail, rain and wind came on! This time we were out for a good 20 minutes before getting totally drenched. The wee fella was in really good spirits despite the snow and hail lashing against his face as I ran with him on his bike back to the car.

I managed to fit in some yoga practise in preparation for tonight's session. Robbie got to watch a fair bit of his Cars movie.

David came home about 1pm for a shower... he was full of jokes and excitement – I felt I couldn't share this as I was feeling so emotional this time round. We had a good wait of 40 minutes and then we saw our bouncing little baby... it was more amazing than I can ever remember and I just wanted to sob my heart out with happiness! David said he felt a wee tear too. I can't explain how emotional I felt this time to see this little baby doing back flips and moving so much. I now really feel like I've got a little person growing inside me.

The midwife had to do her detailed consultation which went through all my previous pregnancies, and to take bloods etc. All was fine and she suggested I would be ideal for a home birth if I wanted! Well, this lit my face up as I had even mentioned this to David last week after our neighbours not so happy time in the hospital ward during the night after having her baby. David is really not up for it but the midwife has left it open for us to think about for a while. Apparently they bring the 'home kit' out two weeks before the due date and the midwives are on call for this period of time before and after the due date.

After the hospital, we picked up the kids and shared our good news. Jane and Robbie were so, so excited, it was so lovely to see. Jane said she wanted a little sister and Robbie wanted a little brother and wanted to see him in my tummy now! It's going to be a long six months for them! Jane is so excited, she wants to tell everyone tomorrow... the whole school is going to know by the end of tomorrow!

I took my jogging group and yoga class tonight – both went well though I was tired and drained from the excitement, I would have loved a night off. When I came home, David was in the process of putting an update on Facebook! I quickly sent a private message to the clients that didn't know and some friends in case anybody wrote a message on my wall. Nobody did and to be honest, I wish I had been able to write a message however I feel really sensitive to my sister and client who are trying for a baby. I will put a wee message on at the weekend.

Thursday, 8th March

Well, Jane had her great news to spread around the playground this morning – I almost felt like I wanted to hide!

Robbie and I had a bit of a lazy morning – he was sticking and pasting and I was tidying up and eating lots. Bought more carbs at the shop this morning – bagels, white rolls and Philadelphia light! It's not brilliant but it seems to be what my body needs. I am much hungrier in the mornings – that's for sure. I also bought fresh orange juice as I've had a wee notion for this.

Out on the bike with a client this afternoon – this was good. Although it's a thought to go to work, I do enjoy the outdoors and fresh air once I'm there. I am feeling increasingly tired and emotional again these last few days.

My friend came over for tea and a catch up tonight. We had a cheese and tomato pizza – the first pizza in months that I've felt like eating. She isn't in a relationship at the moment and hasn't got kids, but she's in a really good place with her life just now. Enjoying lots of action holidays and making so many good friends. It was good to see her looking so much happier.

She did mention how I looked like I'd put on weight – on my face! OK so that's two people have said this and it's not really what I want to hear, although she did say it made me look younger. I said I think it's partly with my haircut that my face is looking different as the scales aren't quite saying I've put on weight.

Jane had a bit of a hissy fit at bedtime, asking for water just when the lights went out. She cried for nearly 45 minutes while my friend was still here… I would normally have just given her a sip of water, but my friend was saying, 'You can't give in to her!' Oh well, looks like a drama in the morning as she was told she wouldn't get her school dinner tomorrow if the crying continued.

I think David must've been working till about 11pm tonight – away since just after 6am! It's good he's getting the work but he's going to exhaust himself.

Friday, 9th March

Well sure enough we didn't have a good start to the day as Jane remembered she wouldn't get a school dinner. She pleaded and pleaded but we were firm and she eventually accepted it. David took all the girls to school this morning for a change, as I'm quiet with clients later, I said I'd take Jane swimming. Jane was delighted at this.

I had the bags ready to go swimming with Robbie this morning and he chose to go to the park on his bike instead. Fine with me! The fresh air was what I needed but I've been waking up with a very sore head and earache. Not really great having a cold at the moment.

Well, I had a lovely outdoor session with my client once Robbie went to nursery. Work was really quiet for a Friday but I'm making the most of it! I went for a swim after this and really, really enjoyed it; the sun was coming in through the windows and making patterns on the bottom of the pool. It felt so peaceful and calming and I'm going to do a lot of swimming again during this pregnancy. I left feeling like I'd had a facial and a great bath! I picked up Robbie from nursery and then Jane from my pals. Jane was meant to go to a swimming lesson tonight however her behaviour and cheek to me was way above board. I simply asked her to get changed from school clothes and put her clothes in the washing basket and she was starting to grunt and say she hated me!

I really have had a lot of this over this week and I've had enough. I just walked away as I was so upset and feel like I might end up screaming at Jane. Not good for anyone, especially not how I felt the other night. So no swimming. She cried for a while in her room and then accepted the decision. She said sorry and sat on my knee while I read a book. A much calmer resolution. I need to walk away and compose myself more often.

David came home early because I asked if he could, in light of the situation, and I'd thought it was going to get worse. She's been good as gold since dinner but she'll be getting a telling from her Dad later.

Looks like a chilling out night for me again – David heading back to work after dinner.

Saturday, 10th March

Usual Saturday, circuits then antenatal yoga and then a client for jogging. It was a lovely day though cold and windy. I loved putting the girls through their paces and my client did brilliantly with jogging three miles in 35 minutes. I have been feeling quite rough though with headaches and I don't want to be taking painkillers in case it's something I shouldn't ignore.

When I came home from work I was starving. I enjoyed every bit of my chicken baguette with Philadelphia and managed some spinach and pepper, so I believe I am getting a little bit healthier! Though David did his usual and bought delicious cookies – I had a bit more than one and less than two! They were lovely.

I had to have a lie down this afternoon as my head and right eye were pounding. I should have got up after 20 minutes but I literally felt like I couldn't get back up. I stayed in bed for over an hour and then David went to the shops with Robbie. Jane didn't want to go and wanted to stay at home and colour in. I had a bubble bath and once again didn't want to get back out! It's a good job I was active this morning as I've felt like a lazy bum all afternoon.

I checked my blood pressure tonight as I'm starting to worry about the headache and pre-eclampsia. It was 120/74 which is a little higher for me but totally normal. I think if I still feel rough in the morning I will phone NHS 24. My mum is coming to visit tomorrow as I said I am struggling a bit with the headaches.

David made a lovely seabass dinner tonight, a real effort. I'm pretty much done in and its only 9.30pm. Bed is calling me…

Sunday, 11th March

I woke up feeling a lot better. Thankfully, my headache has gone and I got a little lie in till about 7.30-ish. David was up and away early after giving the kids their breakfast.

I got on and did some housework before my mum arrived about 10am.

She brought a lovely spring potted plant for outside the front door and this really cheered me up. We took the kids to the park and went round on the bikes, though Jane was quite huffy and didn't want to go on her bike, saying that her knees were sore. We managed it though without any major upsets.

When we got back we all made our own pizza from scratch – It was lovely, really doughy and filling but I managed to pack away a fair helping! As the afternoon went on I got more and more tired… We all played games together and then I got on with the ironing while my mum played kitchens with the kids upstairs. David came home for dinner – soda scone, poached egg, beans and bacon! It was quite nice and then I desperately wanted some creamy ice-cream and had to settle for the soya option in the freezer.

As it got nearer bedtime I got more and more tired and miserable feeling. In fact, to be honest, I've just felt so low all day. I just can't pick myself up and get enthusiastic about anything. I know it's just the hormones and it should pass soon, but I just feel low. It's a good job I do the job I do as it forces me to get out in the fresh air and get some exercise… not to mention to put a smile on my face and be enthusiastic.

I'm also feeling guilty at how little yoga I am fitting in. I'm yawning my head off just now and it's 8.30pm, but I'm hoping to push myself out of bed in a minute and do at least 30 minutes of self-practice.

Well I did it and I'm so glad I made myself get up and get on with it. Good night!

Monday, 12th March – 14 WEEKS

Today started with me cleaning my ground mats for work before 9am… Might as well try and start the day as I hope to go on! Robbie was out on his scooter and it just felt a bit more like Spring.

Then I met with a yoga teacher that taught the antenatal yoga on my Teacher Training course. We met at a Ceramics Cafe – a lovely little set-up with a small soft-play, café and area for painting and decorating ceramics. Robbie had a great time and it was so nice to speak with her about her challenges with her wee boy Gavin (he's two years old now). I hope to keep in touch and maybe she'll take over my classes on a Wednesday night when the time comes.

I took Robbie to nursery and then I went for a four mile jog – my average pace was 10.30min/mile which is really getting pretty slow however I'm keeping going! I then had a sleep before eating a cous cous stir-fry and heading back out to work. A few more jogs – about 10.30-12min/mile pace… But by now, I am feeling the effects of my earlier run. It's a bit frustrating as I find it hard to do nothing on days when it's good weather and I've got time in the afternoon but know I will be working later.

When I was out with my second jogger I felt I was going to take a bit of a funny turn… the feeling went within about 10 minutes. This worried me as I thought I might end up fainting and this is so dangerous that I'm taking this risk. I kept thinking I'd cancel my last clients but I just kept going as it was a yoga session in their home and they're such a lovely couple. I had a banana and a big handful of mixed nuts and raisins that have been in my car for about a year!

This couple are really enjoying the yoga. The husband is a lawyer and is finding it's helping with his relaxation but also his flexibility and workout in the gym on the Tuesday morning. The wife has had a sore lower back since childbirth and she said after the last session her back hasn't been sore all week. Its great hearing how people benefit. Although this session time isn't ideal for me long term, I'll keep trying to do it going forward as they are doing so well.I came home and had another banana and some soda scone!

Tuesday, 13th March

Looking back on today, it doesn't seem like I've done much or have much of a reason to be feeling the way I am… That is, pretty low, moody and miserable! I did some shopping this morning with Robbie and he was well behaved. Bought lots of bakery bread foods and some mini savoury eggs to go with my Philadelphia cheese late morning time! I also got wheat crackers which I've munched through most of.

I had a client between dropping off Robbie and picking up Jane this afternoon. It was a weights session so again it's not been anything physical for me. I think yesterday and the late night at work just takes its toll on me at the moment. I was a bit short and grumpy with my mum on the phone… Totally unnecessary. She was telling me how she's making her brother, David a tray bake of mars bar crispy cake and I made a comment about how that's not likely to help him much! He is in a physical job with lambing coming up but he's always had a big sweet tooth and he's in his 60s. She made some comment about 'Oh yeah that's right you've done all your nutrition and everything, haven't you?' and 'I'm not getting into this with you just now,' which I thought was a bit over the top for a little comment I made. Anyway she's just wanting to treat him and why shouldn't she… She didn't expect to come on the phone asking about how I was feeling to be made to feel bad about making cakes for her brother! David phoned later too to see how things were and I was the same moody two shoes with him. I could barely muster the energy to talk with him and I was feeling so desperate for a sleep. I ended up having a power nap before dinner and put the telly on for the kids!

Jane has been well behaved all afternoon – she did her homework fine, no cheeky behaviour and ate her dinner. Robbie didn't eat his dinner so he had a few strops but despite going to bed without dinner he didn't throw any major tantrum. He did however fall asleep quicker than Jane which is rare!

So here I am sat in bed by 7.30pm again and struggling to keep my eyes open and struggling to motivate myself to do anything. I've nibbled away at cheese and jam and crackers since dinner and eaten almost a full melon over the course of the day! It's probably got more to do with the fact that I'm eating so many carbs that I'm tired. David is at work and will be till at least midnight so once again I'm feeling like I'm a single parent these days. I do like my space though and I think to be honest, right now with the way I feel it's probably for the best that he's not around as I'm not much company!

I'm thinking about just going to sleep now but I'm meant to take Jane to the toilet about 10pm and the last few nights I haven't managed and she's wet the bed by the time David has come in. I'm thinking I'll just put a nappy back on her!

Wednesday, 14th March

It's been a pretty quiet day with work. Robbie and I just did a few odd jobs first thing in the morning that needed doing and then my sister-in-law visited for a cuppa. This was the first I'd seen her since we broke the news about our pregnancy. It's funny, one of the first things she said was: Was it a surprise?' I think she was equally surprised that no, it wasn't a surprise!! She has one child, who is a month younger than Jane. He loves being with Jane and Robbie and has been asking for a sleepover so she has offered to take them both on the first night of the Easter holidays. I don't really feel up to returning the favour at the moment, but I'm delighted that they have both been asked. She also brought some lovely homemade choc chip cookies – I've probably eaten two of these and am feeling quite guilty about the volume of stodge that I'm eating.

When Robbie went to nursery I went for an hour-long walk before coming home and preparing my yoga class for this evening.

I picked the kids up and got them sorted with dinner and homework… all done without any problems or tantrums. I went out to my jogging group – we all did 30 minutes jogging and then on to the yoga class. It was another successful class, a few new faces and a few more people finding out my news.

I came home and my mother-in-law was here watching the kids for a few hours while David went back to work. He said he'd likely be home by midnight but didn't get in till 2.30am. I was up at the toilet at 2.15am and wondered where the hell he was… Sent a text and in the meantime had all sorts of thoughts going through my head. Overall with two toilet wake-ups and a lot of strange dreams… Take That playing a private gig at my local church hall where I do my yoga class… it wasn't a great night's sleep.

Thursday, 15th March

Hooray, this has felt like a long week since I was going by a Tuesday as my date for "weeks changing" and now, since the scan, it's a Thursday. Despite the poor sleep last night, I've not been too cranky! I took Robbie to the gymnastics club and he met a pal there with his gran.

She was asking what quite a few friends and family are asking, 'When am I going to work up till?'

I went for a swim today when Robbie was in nursery. I'm glad I forced myself to go as it was that or back to bed as feeling tired and also full with food! Ate almost two bagels and a tin of tomato soup for lunch (with some grated cheese, of course!) and then three chocolate roses!! If I let me belly all hang out I would look six months pregnant. Instead I am trying to pull it all in to keep myself feeling leaner for longer. The clothes I wore today were feeling pretty tight though, especially around my chest where I've expanded. I'm going to overhaul my wardrobe I think and try and find clothes that makes me feel good and comfortable.

I picked up Jane and her friend from school and then Robbie from nursery. I made a pot of pasta bolognaise and ate far too much (had second helpings) and then continued to eat some more chocolates… Really no need for it as I was stuffed. Also, I remember in my other pregnancies I really didn't overeat like this and this definitely helped me lose the weight after birth. I'm so aware that you're only meant to consume an extra 200-300 extra calories in the last trimester – but I feel like I've doubled mine!

Well another early night… David came back home for dinner and went out again for "a few hours" – I hope so. It's great that he's getting so many orders but he needs to get someone else working with him.

Friday 16th March

I woke up with Jane coming in having wet the bed… Despite being lifted by David later on. This is proving hard to crack for Jane. I weighed myself this morning as I forgot to do it yesterday – I was eight stone 6lb which surprised me as I thought I was eight stone 3lb last week… I can't be putting on 3lb a week or I really will be massive!

Today at school it is "Eco Day" and the kids were to wear something green and comfortable. Jane was very excited and in a great mood this morning.

I picked up her two friends and took them to school too, then we went to visit my neighbour with her new baby. She is having a hard time of it with Jessica not settling too well in the cot – I can't remember it being quite like that with Jane and Robbie. It's a good thing she's got help with her parents.

Robbie went to nursery and I had only one client this afternoon and I was on my bike for this. Since the session, I have been totally knackered and just wanted my bed. I'm a bit worried about next week as I've got four on Monday and five on Wednesday and the work is just exhausting me. I'm making every effort to eat more fruit (still not drinking enough water and still pretty constipated) and less carbs that make me tired. It's hard as I'm always so hungry in the morning. Today I had my breakfast cereal, two bagels, melon, strawberries and macaroni cheese with the kids tonight after Jane's swimming lesson. Before dinner, I felt so nauseous again and then since dinner I've been almost sick a few times. I'm going to look at my work for tomorrow and get my eyes closed for the night!

Saturday, 17th March

A beautiful day outside and driving to circuits this morning I felt really happy with the world! I had a glass of water with my breakfast and I'm going to continue to do this every morning to help with the bunged up bowels! (it seemed to help!)

I only had two at my antenatal yoga which is really disappointing and I think I may have to cancel this as it's actually costing me money. Then I went to a client's house to do yoga combined with some light weights – this was fun and I like that this is a new dimension to training that I can use.

I only had a banana as a snack this morning so quite pleased with myself for not snacking on the crisps. My tastes have definitely changed a bit over the last week as I'm not needing a fruit corner every day or cottage cheese. In fact I haven't had cheese all day. David made me a lovely chicken roll at lunchtime and then I made another, followed by a yogurt! I carried a bottle of water about with me all afternoon so I've done a lot better with drinking water.

We took the kids to the quiet train station road where there is a closed road and it's perfect for learning to ride the bike. Jane can now ride the bike; it was amazing to watch and I was really emotional with how both Jane and David stuck with it. She mastered it in less than half an hour! It's been great having the four of us all spending the afternoon together. David is now making me a steak stir-fry of sorts! Tomorrow is Mother's Day and though David is working in the morning he's going to finish up about 2pm and we're all going to Di Maggios for dinner.

Sunday, 18th March

Mother's Day and David was away to work at 6am (alarm was set for 5.15… He did offer to make breakfast at this time but I declined!) Once I'd got the kids breakfast, I went back to bed for some chillout time and they both surprised me with lovely cards they made while they were downstairs. Very thoughtful and not even prompted. I am very lucky.

It has been a beautiful sunny day outside and once we got up and going we had a shot of the bikes again. Jane can now start off cycling on her own which is great. It's magic seeing how this has helped her confidence.

After lunch, we headed over to David's mum and dad's and met David there. By then, I was feeling pretty knackered and getting a bit cranky if I'm honest. Nothing much happened there and when we got back we just got ready to go into town to Di Maggio's at Royal Exchange Square. We all had a really enjoyable time as a family – the kids ate great with their pizza and ice-cream… Robbie even picked up the ice-cream glass and drank the last of it! I had a Mediterranean pizza with courgette, aubergine and peppers – it was really cheesy but that's good for me at the moment! I also had two diet cokes which I never have but I really enjoyed my dinner.

It was pretty much bedtime for the kids once we got home. After putting them to bed David suggested I give him a deep tissue leg rub… I'm confused, I thought it was meant to be me getting pampered! I suggested he booked himself in somewhere as I had work to do tonight and yoga to prepare for the week. He was clearly very unimpressed and looking for some attention. I just haven't got the interest or energy at the moment for much loving. Its 8.15pm now and I'm going to get on with the yoga as I've got a busy week ahead. It's unlikely I'll be able to write this journal till Tuesday or maybe Thursday as I've four clients tomorrow finishing at 10pm and then on Wednesday got five sessions booked. It's going to be a hard week.

Monday, 19th March

Well it's true not to waste time thinking about the future. Jane suddenly seemed really clingy and pale in the playground this morning. I felt awful for her but she didn't say what was wrong. I left her at school and a few hours later the school phoned to say Jane had been sick. Robbie and I went to get Jane and she was like a poor wee soul, white as a ghost. She was sleeping by the time we got home and I just placed her in her bed. I had to lift Jane again to take Robbie to nursery and she was quite upset and was sick when we arrived at nursery.

I cancelled my first client and Jane slept again for most of the afternoon. I took Jane to the doctors as her friend has been the same though has also got a chest infection. Jane is OK, just a virus that is going round. I was then starting work at 5pm in Glasgow and starting to feel a bit ropey. The session was indoors which was good since the weather had changed for the worse. On the drive to the next client, I was toiling with the idea of cancelling. I nipped in home to go to the toilet and felt dreadful and looked very pale. I decided to cancel the last session and go to the first one at 7pm. It was a yoga session and went well, though I was glad to be going home. I was right to cancel the last session as I needed the rest. I haven't been sick and my stomach has settled down again… it is frustrating losing £65 of work today for two hours but there's nothing I can do about that now. Early night again.

Tuesday, 20th March

Last night, I was up with both Jane and Robbie – David didn't even know. I'm usually up twice with needing the toilet anyway. Every morning, I wake up with earache in my left ear and headaches. I've been lying on my left side as for a while now it's not felt too comfy on my back or my right side.

Both Jane and Robbie needed some paracetamol and then went back to sleep. I felt a bit bad about suggesting Jane go to school today, but she was diving around full of energy and had said she wanted to go. Her temperature was fine at 8.30am and I gave her some more paracetamol before going to school.

Robbie has been a bit irritable today. I don't know if this is just a new phase for him, standing his ground, or if he's not feeling too good either. He cried and whined for nearly half an hour as I asked him to change out of his favourite "Cars" top so he could eat his tomato soup! As usual my patience is great in the morning and afternoon and then as I get more tired withheadaches by teatime my patience is shot.

I had a client at my house for a yoga session today while Robbie was at nursery. It was a good session and she really enjoyed it, what I wasn't expecting was her parting comment that she was shocked to see I was showing a bump so much! I didn't think I was showing that much… Nobody else has really mentioned me having a bump. Well, I am almost 15 weeks.

The kids went to bed really well tonight and I had a pizza all to myself and I have to say I really enjoyed it. This is the second pizza this week though so it's not ideal! David will be in late again tonight… I've looked over my work for tomorrow and going by how I'm feeling with the headaches I'm a bit worried about how I'll feel by the end of tomorrow.

Wednesday, 21st March

Well, today, my poor wee boy Robbie has been really ill with a high temperature. It reached 39.4 which is too high. I felt dreadful but with the combined nurofen and paracetamol I managed to get it down to about 38C. What was worse was that I had to go to work as it was too busy a day to lose. David's mum came over to watch Robbie for the afternoon. He just kept cuddling me and saying, 'Mummy.' So off I went to work feeling really guilty. The day went in pretty quickly and after the third session I had time to pop home and see everyone, get a bite to eat and a shower and go back to work.

Robbie had improved for a few hours but then was starting to heat up again. Robbie was saying how he misses Mummy when she goes to work… He is such a treasure. Jane was saying the same too but David had surprised them with some white chocolate buttons to win them round!

Thursday, 22nd March

15 weeks today! As usual, I was up twice – both with Robbie… Needing medicine and a tissue for his runny nose. I kept up the dosage of medicine and he seemed to be settling and full of energy. We even went to the dentist for a check-up and to repair part of my lost filling. His temperature was at 37.5C and he was keen to go to nursery so I sent him.

It was a beautiful sunny day, the best day of the year so far and I was feeling in need of some quiet time out walking at the park. It would also have been my gran's birthday today and I was feeling a bit upset anytime I thought about her. She died of Ovarian Cancer just months before Jane was born.

Well, I've been feeling guilty about sending Robbie to nursery as his temperature soared to over 40C by teatime. I hadn't given him the nurofen as I thought he was getting better. So he's been agitated and too hot and I think I've got him settled now with both paracetamol and nurofen and a cold flannel. He's in bed sleeping with no clothes on and just a thin sheet over the top of him. I've felt terrible most of the day. I'm going to head to bed after doing another wee temperature check of Robbie. I feel like I've got the flu in my head at the moment.

I have a midwife appointment in the morning for the 15-week blood test and I'm also going to ask for the flu jab. I'm really worried that my baby is being harmed with how I'm feeling at the moment.

Well I phoned NHS 24 as I was so worried about my boy. They phoned back just when David came in from work and saw wee Robbie sleeping in our bed. He had to get seen by the doctor because of his temperature hike, it seemed such a shame to wake him after taking so long to get him to sleep, but he took it so well. The doctor said he was ok. Although a bad virus it doesn't seem to be in his chest and we've to just keep our eye on him.

Friday, 23rd March

Robbie has been better during the night and slept ok, just up once and given medicine. We're keeping him off nursery today… I've learnt my lesson after yesterday! I went to my midwife appointment and it was such a relief to hear that our baby is growing perfectly and to hear the heartbeat loud and clear. Everything else was fine and I've to get my flu jab once my current bug has settled down.

Robbie and I read lots of stories this afternoon and did a little bit of gardening in preparation for our vegetable plot and seed planting.

Jane was dropped off by our friend's mum who advised me there was a note in her book and if I wanted to phone on Monday for a chat, that would be fine. This was on the back of Jane telling me that yesterday, the warmest and best day of the year to be outdoors, that she didn't get out to play at lunchtime. She said she and a friend had to finish work in the classroom. Well, my blood was boiling as I think play is so important to clear the head and make friendships. So I wrote in Jane's book about this and how unhappy I was about it. The craziest thing is that I was speaking to the teacher after school yesterday while we waited outside on her getting ready and she never mentioned it. The disappointing thing for me was when I told David he agreed with the teacher. I've blown off steam to a few friends and everyone else thinks it's crazy that at age five they are kept in over lunchtime.

So, today's note from the teacher said Jane only had three words to copy down and she was surprised it had taken her the whole lunchtime to do this. I'm still very unhappy as I don't think they should have been left unsupervised at all. I will definitely be speaking to her teacher on Monday, oh joy!

I was out at work tonight – a really pleasant night to be outdoors training. My pelvic floor muscles were dreadful though and I was so desperate for the toilet after the first session that this didn't help.

I'm sure I felt the first flutters of life from my baby today, while waiting in the car for my client. It's really starting to feel more real now; my tummy when

I run feels a bit pushed up and uncomfortable. I was hoping to do the Women's 10K in May – I will be 22 weeks by then, and will possibly make this my last run.

Saturday, 24th March

I had a great day. My circuits class was good as I had two new girls come along pretty much last minute. Then I had a cycle with a client doing a seven mile run. I came home and got myself ready for my afternoon at Chillout Yoga West of the Moon where I was going to a discussion on yoga and cancer. This proved so interesting, humbling and worthwhile. This is definitely an area I feel strongly about as apparently more and more people are getting cancer (and more surviving it too) – however it's no surprise when we consider our lifestyle factors nowadays with regard to stress, diet and exercise.

When I got home, my sister-in-law was here with the kids and David. It was a relaxing few hours all together and then David and I had dinner – chicken noodle stir-fry and watched Saturday night telly. I'm sad to say I really enjoyed The Voice and Take Me Out… What's happening to me! Wish I'd gone to bed earlier though as we lose an hour of sleep tonight when the clocks go forward.

Sunday, 25th March

Wow, what a gorgeous sunny day and hot too. I took the kids to Mass this morning (which I barely ever do), as I want to make sure they appreciate what Easter is all about. I'm glad I did as it broke up the morning and gave us something to get up and ready for. .

I came back to find my mum had sent a message saying that she and my sister could come to Jane's gymnastics display after all. This really cheered me up and Jane was very excited. I know my sister was probably feeling anxious about seeing me but it was good to get that out of the way, it's done now. Jane did well though she did seem to be in a bit of a daydream during it, I think her cold has been lingering on.

Mum and I had a lovely afternoon out the back garden with the kids playing. I have felt so much better today and made us all a baked potato with tuna salad for dinner – I'm so impressed that I wanted to eat salad and I've felt much better. I've not been needing the same amount of bread and cheese and dairy as before and after eating a whole bag of mini eggs last night, I'm determined not to have any goodies today.

After the kids went to bed, I did 45 minutes of yoga practice… because I felt like it. This was really nice as I've not been able to fit in much self-practice lately.

Poor David has been working all day today indoors, oblivious (until I told him) of the 18C sunshine temperatures we've had.

Monday, 26th March

Well, what another gorgeous day and I feel so lucky I'm working outdoors. Despite it being hot, I'm feeling pretty good with running. I went a run after my first client and I was running better than I've ran in about six weeks! I was running at 9.30-10min/miles.

The only real downside of the day was the telephone call I had with Jane's school teacher over the issue of her missing a whole lunch break outside last week. It seems she was left unsupervised in class for full lunch break. Apparently, the Teacher only expected her to finish off three words and not the whole blackboard of sentences. Hey, she's five years old and made a mistake! Well, I ended up having a good rant which maybe went on a bit much about other things. I spoke with David about it later and he was very good at listening to the story and giving a non-judgemental perspective. We've got parents night this Thursday and if we can't get someone to watch the kids then, he'll go himself.

The rest of my day was training at Kelvingrove Park and then an hour's yoga teaching to a couple in their home.

Tuesday, 27th March

And another beautiful day. Robbie and I made his Easter Bonnet for his nursery parade on Friday and then we played out in the back garden until nursery time. I had a client today – another session of weights at the park… It's a hard life!

Well I shouldn't joke because it got a good bit harder when I picked up Jane from school with her friend. Jane was just unbelievable. I picked her up and she just looks miserable and grumpy and was so cheeky to us both. We came home and decided to go out on our bikes, all four children and my neighbour with baby Jessica. Well, what a disaster. Jane had one tantrum after the other and was unbearable… screaming and stamping in the street, abandoning her bike and crying at the drop of a hat. I really am struggling with her behaviour and can't understand why it's so bad except the influence of tiredness with school. She will benefit from the Easter holidays. I was surprised that homework was even on the cards but she actually did it really well.

I'm so exhausted, mentally and emotionally with Jane that it's such a thought to do anything once they are in bed. I'm pleased though that I've tidied up and I'm going to get on with the ironing. I've entered the Women's 10K on 13th May too and hope to raise money for the Eve Appeal if I do it.

My eating today has been fantastic (not including the chocolate easter egg that I ate the remains of!). I've had two salads today with avocado and salmon and I'm really happy that this is what my body now wants... Hooray! Breakthrough!

Wednesday, 28th March

Work was fairly quiet so I went for a four mile run in the heat today... Though I stayed in the woods and my average pace was about 10.30min/mile and HR was pretty steady at 146bpm all the way (which is just about 65% of my maximum HR, so all fine there). My later client wanted a session of yoga and toning and a good chat! Then it was the jogging group – first week at the park and only two could make it. The yoga session tonight was quiet too with only eight students, although I'd heard at least five that knew they couldn't make it.

Thursday, 29th March

16 weeks today! Apparently my baby is 11.5cm from crown to rump! I've been feeling so much better this week and wanting to eat much healthier that I sometimes think I'm not pregnant anymore. I have been feeling little movements though when I'm sit quietly which has been so lovely. Also weighing myself weekly now and weighed eight stone 7lbs.

We had a tough night with the kids though, especially with Robbie. He was up at least three times and wide awake – I do feel really tired today. That said, I've had a very lucky day as my friend's mum and dad took Robbie to gymnastics this morning while I had a dentist appointment for a new crown. The dentist offered me the matching "white" crown for £150 instead of £200 (since my usual dentist is a client of mine and he reckoned if she hadn't been on holiday she would have made me this offer).

After picking up Robbie and having lunch it was then time for nursery. I had a walk at the park and then relaxed for a little while in the garden with my new book "anti-cancer"... I also had a wee power nap before picking up the kids.

Then it was parents day at Jane's school – she got an average report. She's a little behind in a few areas and lacks concentration but she is not the worst in the class, and at least this time the teacher didn't come across so dramatic and serious about the matter.

I'm now getting really, really tired and thinking an early night reading my new book is on the cards, in fact I might even have a bath. David is out at a fundraising race night for his sister. I'm going to wait on the ice-cream van and get myself a wee goodie. I know I should have a drink of water but I think I might buy a fizzy drink. Today, I've had another salad and then egg and beans at tea. Overall, I'm much happier with how I'm eating.

Friday, 30th March

Today was a lovely, pleasant day as I only had one client late afternoon and the prospect of the kids having a sleepover at my sister-in-law's was great. It was also the last day of nursery and school for two weeks. I sent Robbie off with his Easter bonnet decorated with a "Cars" theme for his own personal touch. He was delighted.

I had a lovely walk at the park before picking them both up and getting them ready for their Aunt picking them up. It's amazing how I miss them the minute they are in the car and driving away and praying that they are safe and nothing happens to them.

David and I went to Oran Mor for dinner. We were both starving which was great as usually I snack so much I don't notice being that hungry. I had goats cheese to start with followed by braised steak, winter vegetables and mash and then I had a berry crumble and ice-cream to finish! I never normally have three courses but we were feeling indulgent and were just heading home afterwards to watch a DVD.

I didn't see more than 20 minutes of the DVD before falling asleep.

Saturday, 31st March

Circuits was good fun again this morning – four girls turned up which was alright as a few regulars couldn't make it. I then went a run, though my watch kept cutting out and so I did over four miles but wanted to keep going until it said at least four miles! I did this in 42.35 mins, average 10.39min/mile. Thinking this is not bad going as first mile took 11 minutes and my HR average was 141.

I came home and quickly showered before going to pick up Jane and Robbie from their aunt's. Jane wasn't too impressed to see me since she wanted to stay at her cousins for lunch, so this was a bit disappointing. I soon managed to get her to come round and all was well. We all had lunch together and then headed out to get a scooter for Jane, as Robbie got a good one handed down from a friend. We ended up in John Lewis spending £95 on a scooter! Obscene, but this is the "micro-scooter" that the neighbours have got and it is so easy and light for them to use... And it's the same one Robbie got given to him. David then bought Robbie a red remote control car as his Easter treat (and also because his bonus had come in from work).

For dinner, I made lovely seabass and vegetables for David and me and we watched most of the Saturday night trash on the telly.

Sunday, 1st April

David was away early at work and I took the kids to mass for Palm Sunday. I'm doing pretty well with going to mass these days! I then prepared a little picnic lunch and we headed to Pollok country park with the scooters. On the way in the car my new temporary "crown" fell out! I need to be careful as I don't have the time to go to the dentist tomorrow and get it put in again. I really hope I'm not doing damage with the big gap all-round the crown, I'm worried about decay getting in again.

The kids loved the park and were great at riding their scooters. I couldn't believe the speed of Jane coming down the hills and Robbie picked it up really well today too. I gave them a wee treat in the café as I had a sparkling water and a piece of carrot cake.

They both slept on the way back for 15 minutes and I've been knackered too with all the fresh air and fun. I'm writing this just after putting the kids to bed. I want to now do my prep for tomorrow afternoon and then do some yoga, but I'm so tired.

I managed a wee half hour of yoga so pleased with myself.

Monday, 2nd April

Today was a busy day but nothing was going to prepare me emotionally for the news I was going to get. I took Jane to her hearing test at the Royal Infirmary while my Mum watched Robbie. Jane's hearing is fine, it's just been affected by a few colds and build-up of wax. We came home and had lunch with everyone before my mum took the kids for their adventure sleepover.

I felt so sleepy and the prospect of training outdoors most of the day and finishing at 10pm was not one I was relishing in. I fell asleep for 10 minutes in the chair before heading to work. The postman had been and there was a letter from the Royal Infirmary about my recent 15-week blood sample. The result wasn't favourable and said I was in the "high risk" category for Down's Syndrome. I can't quite describe how I felt but shocked and lost come close. I thought for a second about cancelling my work for the day but then thought how useless I'd be sat at home crying and thinking about something I couldn't change. The appointment to discuss the result was for tomorrow at 2pm but I managed to change this to 9am so that I wasn't worrying all day and then I could go and pick up the kids from my mum's. I missed them even more now!

I decided not to tell David till he came in at night as there was nothing he could do and it would only prey on his thoughts all day too. I went to work and gave my work my all. I didn't want to mention it to anyone however one client asked if I'd had my results in yet. I told her as I couldn't lie.

When I told David, he took it a lot better than I thought. He didn't say much but did start to Google the test itself and think about why I was in the high risk category. He said there looked to be a 1 in 150 chance that our baby could have Down's, and he thought that was pretty positive.

Tuesday, 3rd April

Well, once I'd woken up during the night that was me. I couldn't get back to sleep and my mind was racing thinking over and over again about our baby. I was hoping to feel some movements to reassure me but felt nothing. I think I must have seen nearly every hour on the clock. So much for a lie in and a restful night's sleep while the kids were at their gran's!

We went to the appointment and I could see how agitated and worried David had gotten about it. The lab result said there was a 1 in 36 chance our baby could have Downs. This was a real shock for us both as David had thought it was 1 in 150. I asked if others were better or worse or whether what we had was fairly average. The response wasn't that great however some people do get 1 in 2 chance or 1 in 10 chance. We both agreed that I'd definitely not be getting the amniocentesis test and that we would have to wait till the 20 week anomaly scan to see if anything else showed up there. Unfortunately, the nuchal scan offered by other Health Boards is not an option past 13 weeks.

Although I was very upset, I did manage to remain positive and keep everything in perspective. I really think my yoga is going to come into its own over the next 6 months, especially the breathing and meditation. I feel so lucky to have two healthy children that my thoughts are almost *Well why shouldn't I have a high risk result? I'm no different from anyone else.* I believe we are given in life what we can handle and I will rise up to the challenge of being positive and keeping myself healthy, happy and well while I am nourishing and protecting our baby.

I went to Glasgow for a little shop and bought some clothes. I didn't feel like getting measured for bras and I did keep welling up at random times, but I just kept snapping myself out of it and tried to tell myself to stay in the moment.

It wasn't easy telling mum about the result but she was as supportive as ever. We all went out for a nice lunch and then had a few hours at home chatting and playing before I came back home. David is pretty much finished now at his previous employer's and officially self-employed today! He came home for dinner (chicken salad) and it was really nice all sitting together having a great laugh. The kids were on top form and everyone got on great. I feel so blessed. I'm going to do some yoga now and then watch the second part of "Silent Witness" before going to bed. I hope to sleep better tonight.

Wednesday, 4th April

Well, I slept so much better and feel more positive today. I didn't have work till tonight so I had the whole day with the kids. We did lots of Easter crafts in the morning, an ironing and a trip to Morrison's for more salad and lunch! We went out (it was freezing) to the park for a shot on the scooters and then some chocolate mini eggs to nibble!

I'm eating much better, however I'm also having more cakes and chocolate!

My mum sent me a message that she'd explained to my sister and dad about our test results so that I didn't have to explain. Dad phoned this afternoon and I surprised myself how positive and upbeat I was. He seems to have his own troubles at home. I reminded him of what Gran always said as it does seem to help me – 'There are too many sad faces in the world to be just another sad face, even when you are sad it's better to try and smile and get on with life.'

At my yoga class, (it was very quiet with the holidays) I was talking to a student that has been through a tough five years – losing her dad, her mum being ill and now in a home, struggling to have a baby, going through IVF and miscarrying. Eventually, conceiving and then discovering she had breast cancer. She's come out the other side but life hasn't been easy and remembering her difficulties puts any of mine into perspective.

Thursday, 5th April

17 weeks today… I feel like it was just yesterday I was 16 weeks. I'm disappointed I haven't felt more movement as I'd thought I'd felt some movement over this last week or so. My weight is now eight stone 9lbs which surprised me.

What a lovely day with the kids. Started with us all trekking to the dentists for me to get my new crown and Jane have a check-up. Then we had more fun on the scooters before lunch – they've had so much fun already on the scooters. After lunch, we went to the Ceramics Café – I had a special coupon from the newspaper for a 2-for-1 pottery painting. The kids loved it and I sat and had a hot chocolate.

A pretty simple fun day with the kids, more outdoors time at the park and the scooters in the afternoon. I made a spinach and ricotta tortellini with a carbonara sauce for a wee change. This went down pretty well with a little bit of chocolate easter eggs to finish off.

I started to feel a bit ropey and suddenly very tired just at the kids' bedtime. I decided to just go to bed and read my "anti-cancer" book, though I kept nodding off. David was still at work till after midnight.

Friday, 6th April

I was at work this morning with two clients, a total of about six miles jogging at between 10–12.5min/miles. I really am starting to struggle with feeling the bearing down of my baby on my pelvic floor. My first client was the client that asked about my blood results the other day and she was talking again about Down's Syndrome. Although I'm acting very positive about the future, I really can't bear thinking that this could be ahead of me in our lives and really would like to switch off that thought altogether.

I picked up the kids from my sister-in-law's and then back to pick up the pottery from yesterday. The kids were so excited with their work it was thrilling to see.

I had a plate of watery carrot and coriander soup and tuna mayo sandwich (it was on white bread and full of margarine). I don't think I'll be buying lunch here again in a hurry. I did leave some flyers for my yoga class though since I really want the Wednesday class to continue to grow.

The rest of the day was fairly smooth. David came home at the kids' bedtime and then made me a lovely steak, potatoes and peas for dinner. I finished this off with some ice-cream and after-eight mints! I'm going to have to stop having sweets every day or I'll really notice a difference in my weight gain.

Whilst he was making dinner, I did a 40-minute yoga practise – I enjoyed this and used more props like the cushions for under my tummy when in cobra and twisting to the open space as opposed to the normal side you would twist to.

Saturday, 7th April

Well, circuits this morning was good fun – there were five girls which is a good enough turn out. It seems to be different people every week at the moment that can make it. I came home and wasn't too impressed with David giving the kids chocolate before it was even 9.30am – as he left for work he said, "Mum's being a crabbit git" in front of the kids. I was really hurt and disappointed that he could say something like this in-front of the kids, especially since I am having trouble with Jane saying I'm rubbish or stupid or that she hates me. Really thoughtless of David.

I did the supermarket shop so that David could go to work and have tomorrow, Easter Sunday off. After lunch, we went round to friends for an Easter egg hunt – Jane and Robbie behaved really well thankfully, as they had been warned before going that I wasn't going to put up with any cheek or tantrums.

I had a pretty relaxing night, David worked till after 10pm so we all had a pizza dinner for easiness. I read my running magazine – it was actually quite good this month – though I plan to cancel the direct debit next week as I often struggle to find time to read it. Heading off to bed now at 10.20pm.

Sunday, 8th April

Easter Sunday and David has taken the day off. I started the day with a six mile run and felt great. This is the best I've ran for weeks – my pace average was

10.12 min/mile though each mile was faster than the last. My heart rate max was 150 and mostly at 140 so kept well under control. I'm so happy I've been able to do this as it wasn't difficult. Hopefully the 10K in May is still a goer.

We all went to church this morning. David and I were still not getting on our best as I feel he's undermining me a few times with the kids – he keeps giving them chocolate after breakfast which I know is no big deal but it's after me telling him they've not to get any as they'll be getting lots of goodies later. He then cracked a joke about my new dress – which normally would have been funny but after his comment yesterday morning I still hadn't forgiven him. He said, 'I like your new top… I'm sure my mum had a tablecloth like it when I was young!' Such a comic. This joke was brought up many times later on in the day when all the family were over for Sunday dinner.

My mum, David's parents and his sister were all there. It was a great wee afternoon and the kids behaved well. David made a delicious lamb casserole and we had apple or rhubarb pie with ice-cream to finish us off!

My brother also phoned later tonight and we had a good catch-up.

Monday, 9th April

Today has seemed like a long day with the kids. I didn't leave the house really and I think this is why. The kids played on their scooters while I cleaned my car inside and out. I had a short notice cancellation which was annoying as it's a popular time slot and despite trying three other clients, no-one could make it because it was short notice. I really hate to charge people however this was down to forgetfulness and no fault of mine.

I only had my jogging client – 3.5miles at about 12.30min/mile pace and then my yoga with a couple in their home. It's not much but it's more the fact that it's in the evening that I find hard. I'd love to work just in the mornings! I've also been feeling a little low in mood the last few days. Trying to shake it off.

Tuesday, 10th April

Today has been a good day. I had my first ever flu jab this morning. A quick visit to the shops and bank with the kids then home for lunch. Another big salad for me – tuna today with all my usual trimmings! I ate the rest of the oat and raisin cookie but managed to resist the chocolate today.

We went to a soft play this afternoon where the kids met their friends and I had a good catch-up with my neighbours. They're really struggling with the new baby; it's actually scaring me a bit as they at least have each other helping and I'm fully expecting to have a lot less support.

I made a fabby meatballs bolognaise for me and the kids – they ate really, really well… even Robbie! I think I ate too much though and have felt pretty tired and sluggish all night. I didn't even muster up much energy to do my yoga practise but instead followed a sequence by Esther Eckhart on YouTube. It was fine, though I am feeling like I need to modify my forward bends and naturally my back bends. It looks like tomorrow I'm going to have to prepare my practise for tomorrow night's class while the kids are about. I've had a PT cancellation for tomorrow that I was almost expecting. A client's mum hasn't been well for a while with cancer and I just had a feeling over the last few days that things were maybe not going to be so good.

I'm heading for my bed, David's been at work since about 7.30am and said he'd be back by 10pm – I've just heard him at the door now at 10.15. Another long day for him too.

Wednesday, 11th April

The weather was rotten this morning and so we just took our time getting ready this morning. This is what I love about the school holidays – not having to be ready and dressed for a certain time. This morning the kids were great, playing together and drawing downstairs while I did 45 minutes of yoga practise and preparation for tonight's class.

This afternoon we met with friends at the park and the weather was beautiful, sunny and warm. I started off with my big winter feather down coat, then took off my cardigan and just had a vest top on! The kids had ice-lollies in the back garden!

I had a smashing healthy lunch of salmon and roasted pepper stuffed with cous cous and apricots and cheese, and salad. It was delicious. I'm pleased I am eating good food these days. Though I overdid it on the kids Easter eggs after this healthy lunch!

My jogging group went OK – I say just OK since my bladder control was a problem and I needed to find the nearest bush. The faster part of the group went the wrong way which wasn't good; though they preferred this I would rather I could see everyone.

Yoga was a great session, with ten students, I was happy. The room was like an oven though and my face must have been like a beetroot… It certainly felt like it! I came home and had a bowl of muesli for supper.

Thursday, 12th April

18 weeks today and I've definitely been feeling a good bit more movement from our baby. I've not really been thinking about the high risk result. It's always there at the back of my mind but the reality is that I really don't think it's real. I just know I'm going to be a mess at my 20 week scan. I weighed eight stone 9lbs again today, though everyone is now saying they can see I have curves and see I'm taking shape. A comment at yoga last night… 'I think this is the first I've seen you not looking like you've got a boy's figure… you've got nice womanly curves!' I told this to David and he laughed saying he'd just noticed a big difference last night too.

Today I went to the shopping centre with the kids to get birthday presents for cousins. I needed a nap today, I felt totally exhausted after coming back from the shops. We then planted the seeds in our vegetable garden – I did this fairly randomly, so I'm not sure how these are going to turn out!

The kids were on their scooters again for a while and then Jane had her pram and teddy out – she packed a bag of things she would need for her baby… a cushion, blanket, "sweets" and she'd sat her teddy on top of the potty in the pram in case she peed herself when she was sleeping. What a laugh!

Well the laughter soon ended in tears as I endured a belter of a tantrum from Jane at teatime. Neither of the kids wanted the chicken fajitas I'd made, however Jane took her tantrum to another level… screaming and roaring at the top of her lungs. I just can't manage this behaviour well at all and refuse to tolerate it. She was sent to bed just after 5.30pm and she fell asleep! I've never sent her to bed but I just thought, wait a minute, my parents would never have tolerated that and I'd probably have been sent to bed too. My heart rate was racing and I felt really sad at all the hostility and anger between us.

She woke up when I was giving Robbie a bath and I let her join us. It was nice to end the day in a positive way with resolving chat and cuddles about the event and what we can both learn from it. I hope so. I worry about the stress hormones affecting this baby too.

Well, I'm heading for a bath myself now and a read of my book. I can't even be bothered to switch on the telly. David has phoned and said he'd be home much later. At least we have some precious time away together at weekend and boy am I looking forward to it!

Friday, 13th April

I've had a busy wee day – starting the day with a 45 minute yoga session while the kids drew some brilliant pictures… It's amazing what a new set of felt tips can do for their motivation! We then got ready and got on with the weekly shop. The kids were dropped off at their Gran's only to be told that she was taking them to ASDA! Poor souls.

I had a few clients today… weather was good for outdoors weights sessions and one client running in the evening for four miles. My bladder is not doing too good and I'm constantly having to use people's toilets. I'm finding it much harder running in the evening… My blood feels more sluggish and takes a wee while to get going if I don't fit in a good warm up. My heart rate went up quite high with the running tonight even though it was about 10min/mile. It soon settled down but it unsettled me.

I also fitted in a swim between clients… I'm trying to fit in as much as I can while I'm still comfortable. I did 60 lengths of front crawl and felt pretty good, drinking water every 10 lengths.

David and I enjoyed a supermarket Chinese takeaway for dinner. I've sat doing work preparation for the last hour on the PC, it looks like I might be able to start up the antenatal yoga classes again in a couple of weeks which will be great.

Saturday, 14th April

Circuits was great this morning in the sunshine and the girls worked really hard. I tried to go a run myself after it and disappointedly managed very little. My legs were heavy and tired and I had no energy in me at all… I'm hoping this isn't me running out of steam already! I managed only 2.5 miles in 30 minutes, averaging a pace of 11.30min/mile. It just shows how each day can be different – only a week ago I was almost a 1.5min faster and feeling pretty comfortable. My heart rate was also up higher at about 160 so I really had to be careful.

Once I was home, we all mucked in and got on with the housework before my sister-in-law arrived to watch kids for the night. David treated me to an overnight stay in Glasgow… a five star hotel, a beautiful spa and a pregnancy massage which was just divine. I was a little worried about the massage as the therapist had me lying on my tummy for a bit. She asked if I was comfortable and apart from my boobs being a bit sore I was fine. Also the bed was heated and it got really warm. I started worrying that maybe our baby would over-heat and that I was squashing it – I didn't think you were meant to lie on your tummy at all once you had a bump. Well, baby was moving around a lot initially and then stopped and it was then that I decided to mention it! She reassured me it was OK and switched the heat off the bed. I'm glad to say that baby moved around later again today!

We had a really good dinner in the hotel – I had a cleanser salad starter, though really only because most of the other starters had either shellfish or liver in them. It was delicious anyway and then I had a half duck and chips (which weren't that great), followed by a sticky toffee and date pudding with plain ice-cream (it was meant to be rum and raisin but I didn't fancy that). I had two lovely non-alcoholic cocktails (at a fiver each!) I couldn't believe the bill came to £122! David didn't see the service charge already added and added more… I wasn't impressed as I feel he is being a bit flash with cash, and while I know he's generous with money I'm more cautious. I also did feel a little guilty about the extravagance of the stay and how maybe that money could have bought some baby things! How sad… But I really did appreciate it.

We were absolutely shattered after our dinner and went straight to bed!

Sunday, 15th April

For some reason, I didn't sleep well last night… A combination of being too hot and thinking about the amount of money we'd spent! David was the same, he said he'd woken up and started to think about work.

Breakfast was lovely – delicious fruit and muesli to start followed by a boiled egg and soldiers. The pink grapefruit juice was very refreshing… I'll need to get some!

We went back to the spa for an hour which was great and then after checking out we went to the shops. We both bought something and headed home. I had my first Starbucks this year – my old favourite, a decaf soya Caramel machiatta to take-away. I must've saved a little bit this year on Starbucks alone!

It was great getting home and seeing the kids again – they were in good form and David spent most of the afternoon playing football with them and letting them play with their friends out the front.

I did a little half hour of yoga practise, I was just so tired and feeling a bit sick and have heartburn too (probably all the grapefruit juice!). I did some sun-salutations, the salute to the moon sequence, tree pose and upright big toe sequence, a seated gentle twist and the bridge. I felt my pelvis quite tight so was very careful tonight. Also, I didn't spend too long in relaxation as the stinky smell of my mat put me off! I will need to give it a clean!

Well, tomorrow it's back to the routine of school and nursery and David has gone back out to work tonight!

Monday, 16th April

Well that's the holidays over. Everyone got right back into the routine without any bother today. I changed my client's times around to try and space them out a little instead of them all being later in the evening. I did 3.5 miles with my first client after lunch time and really struggled with my pelvic floor muscles. I think I might have to stop running very soon. My next client cancelled once again less than an hour before the session – really disappointing as this time slot is sought after but with that short notice I can't fill it. I then had to wait till my last session at 8.30 pm – I'm totally fine when I get there but it's such a thought waiting to work at that time of night when I'm getting tired.

Tuesday, 17th April

It's great to have a day off thinking about work altogether. Robbie and I had a good wee morning out and about at the library and then the "Ceramics Cafe" before coming home and discovering I'd left the front door of the house open all morning. I must live in a good neighbourhood as any thief could have nicked my laptop and watch within 10 seconds if they'd came into the house!

I enjoyed a long walk in the woods this afternoon while the kids were at school and nursery and was lucky enough to watch and film five beautiful deer grazing in the forest. I started to think of them as being like us… A family of five soon!

I had a good afternoon with the kids and made a large pizza and salad for tea followed by chocolate (too much) and the second part of "Silent Witness". I plan on trying some yoga before bedtime.

Wednesday, 18th April

All I can think about is that in one week's time we will be getting the anomaly scan and I'm quite worried about it. Apart from this, I had a quiet time at work this afternoon so I just went out a short walk and then came home to prepare for yoga in the evening.

I picked Jane up from school and took her to the park on her scooter for a while before going to Robbie's parents night late afternoon. I'm so proud of him as he seems to be really happy and has settled in well to his new nursery. The keyworker thought he was doing very well with everything so I'm delighted.

I had my jogging group tonight – running for 40 minutes tonight, they all did brilliantly. My pelvic floor hasn't been as bad which is a relief though I did put my tena lady on! There were two new girls too which was good as a few couldn't make it. My yoga class was quiet again with only seven… I hope it doesn't get much less particularly since Tracy will be taking the class next week.

I had my first pot noodle in about 25 years tonight out of pure convenience! It wasn't too bad I hate to admit. I haven't felt much movement in last day or so and I'm a bit worried.

Thursday, 19th April

Well, I'm 19 weeks today and weight is eight stone 10 and ¾ lbs! Last night a few of the girls were commenting on my bump. Here's the range of comments… I think I'd better get used to it! "You're putting on the podge", "Oh, you've got a wee bump now" and the nicest was "You just look like you've had a big dinner!".

Robbie and I went swimming this morning and then picked up some things at Sainsburys. Bought sticky buns and some healthy "ready meal" type of food that took my notion! David is away overnight with work and I'm quite looking forward to not being woken later and just having the bed to myself. How bad is that!

My friend came round once the kids were in bed and we had a magic wee catch-up. She's single but doing a fair bit of dating, mostly from online, and having little success in meeting men that don't lie about something up front. It's another reminder of how lucky I am and I think I sometimes need reminded. I was a bit of a greedy pig tonight, though don't feel the slightest bit guilty! I had a healthy big chicken salad when the kids were having their baked potato with cheese and beans, and later shared a sticky iced current bun. When my friend left I had another full one!

Well I was a bit later in bed tonight than I'd hoped for and think I'd just gone to sleep when Robbie was up with a dream, saying his mouth was sore. After a wee cuddle, he went back to his own bed and back to sleep no problem… Until he woke at 5.50am full of beans!

Friday, 20th April

I took the kids to school early to get them involved in the "walking bus" – just as it suggests – we walk to school in a big line. My yoga friend came round this morning and we had such a great wee catch-up… It's been about four months since I'd seen her and I'd doubted she was really keen to meet up at all. She's had a lot of health worries and work demands and it was great to see her; hopefully we'll keep in touch much better in future.

I had a few clients this afternoon, though have suddenly felt really pregnant with the heaviness of the baby bearing down. My first session was a weights/circuit style session and my next two were mostly jogging. I guess in total I've done about seven miles. The second client was a bit faster than the first, around 11 minute miles, though with a hilly route – my heart rate was totally fine, as was my pelvic floor which was a relief. My lower legs keep feeling like they are seizing up like a dead weight though and this concerns me – I believe it's more the time of day and that they are feeling like they need to be elevated – also with my weight gain this is changing the dynamic of my alignment. I'm pleased with myself though and feel good that I am able to keep so active. I've missed having a swim this week though so hope to fit this in next week.

It was good to see David again after his stay away. He made a lovely big omelette with salad for dinner and I finished this off with a substantial amount of dark chocolate with ginger! Oh dear…

I'm looking forward to a weekend off (except the circuits tomorrow which I love) and time with the family.

Saturday, 21st April

Circuits was quiet this morning but still a lovely sunny hour considering how the weather changed later. I had a four mile walk in the woods after it which I loved though I did find it quite hard by the end of it!

I came home to an empty house which was nice… David was doing the weekly shop with the kids after Jane's gymnastics class. I fell asleep on the couch until they came back. I've been so tired all day that I've been glad David was around as a buffer with the kids. Our little baby has been really active today which has been really reassuring for me.

We all went to a Country Park this afternoon and had a great wee time out walking along the nature trail and letting the kids play in the park.

The rest of the day was just great family time and in the evening I fitted in a sneaky wee half hour of yoga while David made the kids dinner. We later had a TV dinner of chicken pasta and then a piece of chocolate roule (it wasn't that nice).

I've got really twitchy legs tonight despite lying on the couch with my feet up for most of the night. I'm heading to my bed at 10pm… Looking forward to watching some of the London Marathon tomorrow – I know a few people doing it this year.

Sunday, 22nd April

Had a lovely slow start to the morning and David got the kids breakfast before going to work. I managed to get the kids interested in the London Marathon on the telly and watched this off and on for a few hours in between reading and doing jigsaws. I was so emotional watching the second and third male racing to get second place and then again when Nell McAndrew finished under 3 hours! It definitely got me wanting to do another one though I'm still not interested in London as it's so big… Though it is pretty flat.

We all went to the park on the bikes and scooters for a short while before lunch and then spent most of the afternoon outdoors, despite Robbie having a bad cough and cold. It was hilarious when they were playing in the back garden and ended up having a bit of a water fight with small buckets of water. I just happened to look out the window when Robbie was trying to soak Jane and threw the bucket of water over himself. I think he got a big shock but he didn't complain since he knew he shouldn't have been doing it!

We were then up at our neighbours for a while so this was great for them. Everyone was pretty well behaved though Robbie was a little whiny with his cold. I feel like I've just grown and grown and grown over the last few days… and feel the baby is really high up too. They were talking about how her baby isn't too great at sleeping unless she's being carried or rocked to sleep and how on the other hand, her sister's baby is really sleepy and almost docile. We were thinking that maybe as she was always on the go when she was expecting that her baby was used to moving around and this helped her sleep well when she was in her mum's tummy. We had a laugh because we're thinking if this is the case then God help my baby!

I had a baked salmon salad for dinner and a little bit of the chocolate roule with the kids. I've now arranged for the antenatal yoga to start again next Saturday too…I just need confirmation from the Minister at the church.

I'm going to do some yoga now in preparation for work tomorrow night too.

Monday, 23rd April

I can't believe I've been back to the supermarket already after David's big shop on Saturday, when he managed to forget a few essentials. I bought in more fruit and also some smoked mackerel for me tomorrow night when he'll be at work.

Robbie is loaded with the cold so we didn't spend long outside before he went to nursery. He's such great company and I just love my time with him at this age – he has the cutest and funniest little facial expressions and comes out with the silliest things. Instead of a body warmer, he calls it a "bobby warmer" which has us all in hysterics.

On my way back from dropping off Robbie, I had a call from the school that Jane had just had a bad fall in the playground and a bang to her head and skint knees. They said she seemed OK but they need to let us know as she banged her head. I felt a wee bit guilty about not going to check on her but advised if she had any other worrying signs of a head injury to get back in touch. A friend picks Jane up on a Monday and later sent a text saying she was neither up nor down… Phew.

I had a busy day with four sessions – the first one was a weights session outdoors in lovely sunshine and within minutes of finishing the session the heavens opened… Lucky me again! My next client in Glasgow was half indoors doing boxing/circuits and then a 15 minute jog – so all went well. By the time of the next session, I was really feeling the need to go to the toilet. I managed to continue jogging for four miles (took about 50 minutes), pace around 12.30 min/ miles. Pleased enough with that and the weather held out for us. My last client was a yoga session and this also went well, but jeez it's a long day when you don't get in till 10pm. I had a bit of writing up to do too so I didn't get to bed till after 11pm.

Tuesday, 24th April

I met up with friends at a new soft play and the kids had a ball. It was magic that we could all have uninterrupted conversation for that length of time! It really does get a lot easier, but then it's going to get a lot harder again for me!

I spoke with the guy that runs the place about doing yoga there and he was really keen, especially on the yoga for children or yoga with parent and child. It's planted a little seed, and my little head will keep thinking up new ideas for the future after my baby arrives.

Robbie went to nursery and I had a client at the park – another weights session which went well. It's turning out to be a busy week. The busier I am, the quicker time passes – if it could go any faster.

After collecting Jane from school, we had the usual routine of homework, dinner, bath and bed. I ate my mackerel salad and really didn't enjoy it… I won't be having that again for a while. Then I decided I should have some ice-cream to treat myself and despite thinking it was too creamy and sickly, I had a second bowl!

I'm feeling shattered now and it's after 9pm. I'm going to have a pink grapefruit and go and read my book on the inspirational Jane Tomlinson who did an amazing amount of fundraising before dying of cancer.

Wednesday, 25th April

Well today is the day we have our 20-week anomaly scan and I thought I'd be more anxious than what I actually feel. Robbie and I spent most of the morning out and about doing odd jobs so the morning flew in. I had a client booked for straight after dropping him off at nursery – a weights session, outdoors of course, and I got soaked in the rain. Fortunately, I had a change of clothes with me as David was meeting me at the Park for us to head over to the hospital together.

This time, we didn't have to wait that long. A newly qualified midwife did the scan with her colleague there to supervise. It took a while as it would appear that our little baby was trying to hide. The nurse had to really manipulate my stomach to try and get the info she needed. It was a little painful and eventually they wanted me to lie in a decline position on my back, on my side and then to do what I call "the bridge" and wiggle my bum about! David suggested I do a headstand! The little one's heart vessel and chambers are all working brilliantly and everything suggested a good indication of health. There is nothing now to contemplate as this is about all we can go on now till birth time. The only thing for it is to put the blood result to a faraway place in my mind and get on with being positive.

It has been a real relief. We talked about it with Jane and Robbie and read a new book about "Mummy has a house in her tummy"; they both got very, very excited.

I was back out at my jogging group tonight. Not before David made a flyaway comment about how I stack the dishes on the draining board and how it really annoys him. Well, I could feel the rage building inside of me since I do so much that goes unnoticed and he still feels the need to comment on how the dishes are stacked. Let's say my jogging group tonight served two purposes really well – getting out the house into the rain and wind was a pleasure! I also felt quite light and full of energy. My heart rate didn't go much above 150bpm and I was running easily tonight at 9.30 – 10.30 min/mile. I had the group do 3 x 10 min intervals and they were to try and work at a higher intensity. It was a really good session with six joggers.

I came home and had pizza – no yoga for me tonight as I'd prepared for Tracy to take my class in case the scan wasn't too good. I'm feeling the benefit of finishing early and coming home and relaxing. David has ignored me since I came home! I've spent most of my time on LinkedIn and am hoping to make new contacts that might even showcase my pregnancy and fitness. I think I'm in a really positive mood tonight. Off to watch The Apprentice on telly.

Thursday 26th April

20 weeks today, halfway point… it's going in so fast. I weighed eight stone 12lbs this morning.

I've been quite lucky today. My pals' parents wanted to take Robbie to play with his pal at gymnastics so I had a few hours in the morning to myself. I decided to go for a swim though I feel loaded with the cold and can't stop sneezing. Took two paracetamol and just got on with it. I felt much better after the swim, though I was falling asleep reading to Robbie after lunchtime!

After dropping Robbie off at nursery I had a meeting in Starbucks with anetworking guy selling "Nu Skin". Apparently works wonders on everything from ageing, scarring, stretch marks, cellulite and tummy tightening after having a baby. It is pretty interesting but I'm not sure how I could convince David, or even if it really fits in with what I'm trying to achieve with clients. I'll keep it on the back burner just now but if it keeps coming back to my mind then maybe I ought to test the water and see how much interest there is in it.

I managed to fit in an ironing while Jane and Robbie played together. We all had baked potatoes for dinner – I had tuna mayo, cheese and beans. I also bought a carrot cake today, not that I need it!

Tonight, I really should be preparing for my antenatal yoga class starting up again on Saturday and doing some of my own yoga practise, but I am feeling really sleepy. Last night's yoga class with Tracy went very well from what I hear, though again there were only seven students. I'll keep trying to promote this and hope it grows over next few months.

Friday, 27th April

I've been yawning all morning and just feeling all round tired. Went round the park with Robbie on his bike after the school run and then chilled out at home. In fact, I needed a power nap before taking Robbie to nursery as I was falling asleep reading him a story again! So, I parked him in front of the telly… which he loves, while I slept for 20 minutes.

My first client was just after 1pm and we ran 4.5 miles – my heart rate was up a little higher initially and I had a slight feeling of heaviness in my calves as though I couldn't get the blood flowing there fast enough. The pace averaged at under 11 minute/mile but I felt pretty tired. Later, I had another jogger, and even though slower, my body really has been tired and HR was still up a bit more than I'd prefer. We ran for 40 minutes and this was another three miles, so in total today I've ran for 7.5 miles. My last client was at 6pm and an outdoors weights session – I really enjoyed it, though was desperately glad to get home and eat and relax.

David made a lovely chicken noodle stir-fry and we had great hopes for spending a bit of time together until those hopes were dashed (in my opinion) by David! Despite being tired all day and doing a physical job, I'm apparently not allowed to use the "excuse" that I'm pregnant and play on it to request that he puts on another washing and hangs one up! I had said I was wanting in bed before 10pm and this was at 9.30pm and I still had work to prepare for tomorrow. I was not impressed at the look and attitude I got and he suggested that if I can run that distance I can get on with all the other stuff.

I said, 'Would you prefer if I was a lazy, fat slob of a wife that sat about pregnant all day doing nothing, and that I am simply trying to do my job?' I was raging, let's say, to put it mildly. I stormed off to bed in a bad mood thinking he doesn't realise how good he's got it, having a wife that looks after herself and is physically fit enough to do everything that I do.

Saturday, 28th April

I woke up with the memory of last night and was still not impressed; no sign of an apology and I'm not about to back down. I don't want disagreements as we see little enough of each other.

This morning circuits was quiet but still fun in the sun, and they all worked really hard. My antenatal yoga group started and six turned up which was great – they all seemed to really enjoy it.

I then had a client that was doing an 11 mile training run for her first half marathon in two weeks' time – she did great, it took just about two hours and I was on my bike. It didn't feel like two hours.

When I got home, the family were still out playing and I had the chance to eat most of my chicken salad in peace. I have been shattered all day though and am in bed on a Saturday night at 9pm (also to avoid the trash on the telly that David is watching). We had bangers and mash for dinner and then I had a cookie and milky coffee for supper! I really am eating more cakes and goodies than I want to be however I know I need the calories with the amount I am burning off with my job. My baby seems to like all the food and it's lovely even sitting here as I type and feeling lots of little movements. Jane keeps assessing my tummy and giving it kisses, all while being really gentle when she's talking to the baby.

Sunday, 29th April

Well this is a day off, and I started the day with this mindset, as I knew I'd likely be tired. I definitely have a head cold shared by my lovely children. However, once I was up and moving, I just wanted to get stuck into the housework. As the kids were trashing their bedroom and having a great time, I got on with cleaning all the bathrooms including mopping all the floors, putting on countless washings, putting them away, doing an ironing, hoovering, doing dishes… The list goes on. In fact, I actually made a list to show just how much I get through… as much for myself as to show David! He barely said anything about it when I showed him and again he had a look of "well, that's your job". I'm not too impressed as I would like to feel more appreciated. I do think I work really hard with doing a physical job, regardless of whether I love it or not, while at the same time being pregnant.

David ended up with a ticket for the last Old Firm game this year, and I had a bit of it on the telly this afternoon too. His team won 3-0 so I really thought David might have been persuaded to go to the pub and have a drink, but no, he drank soft drinks and bought a curry on his way home. It is good he's had a bit of a day off work though.

I watched a really interesting programme I'd recorded all about breakthrough medicine for cancer treatments. It was phenomenal, using robotics to administer chemotherapy and also to perform surgery. Incredible.

Monday, 30th April

I can't quite believe this is the last day in April today. It is baltic outside and the wind is bitter. I feel so tired and loaded with the cold that I'd have liked to just hide under the covers. Instead, I'm still wearing my big winter coat, gloves and scarf.

I phoned my mum this morning as she'd been away visiting a pal in Aberdeen for the weekend. Turns out she got a bad stomach virus and has been quite poorly. I then took Robbie to a small soft play for an hour – he loved this and was so well behaved. He was trying to be grumpy when we got home, but then decided to break his cover and say he was just trying to be a "wicked wizard" from one of his stories! What a boy.

I had a client right after dropping off Robbie – it was a weights session, and the poor client was also loaded with the cold. I had on two thermal layers and my ski jacket! I hate being cold when I'm standing about – at least it wasn't raining. I had full intentions of coming home and going to bed for a few hours as I was feeling so tired, but I knew I needed to buy some maternity clothes as I'm fed up wearing the same stuff every day. I'm glad I did – some great tops and jeans in sales and so I've got enough to do me just now. I'm going to clear out my wardrobe tomorrow of all the clothes that doesn't fit at the moment.

I had dinner with the kids – fish and vegetables before going to work at 7pm. At least the weather has calmed down and the wind wasn't so bitter. We ran for 4.5 miles and the average pace was just about 13min/mile. This may seem slow, however, the weight on my pelvis has been really heavy tonight, and despite going to the toilet several times before the session, I felt the need to go right away.

My last client was inside doing yoga and this was a lovely session… I just wish it wasn't so late. I think I'll continue with this one for only a few more weeks.

I came home and ate some roasted vegetable crisps and then some toast and an apple. So overall don't think I've eaten any cakes today, oh just remembered I had two wee pieces of milk chocolate earlier today… David would say that doesn't count!

Tuesday, 1st May

Well it's May, and it's looking a little like spring outside, hooray! I've been so, so tired all day, actually exhausted to the point I wonder how I can call myself a Personal Trainer. I did some odd jobs like going to the shops and the bank with Robbie in the morning and then came home wishing for a sleep.

I had a great wee session with a client this afternoon though and then a potential new client approached me during the session looking for advice. I explained my situation and she was still fine with this and getting started even if it is just for a few weeks. She is fairly inactive and so I should be quite alright in doing even a month of training with her.

The kids have been really well behaved today. Jane had her picture taken at school and we had the proof sent home. She is such a beautiful and cute wee girl and I'm so proud of her. We all had fun playing shops and doing jigsaws tonight after dinner. I had a big baked salmon salad for dinner and it was great. A few pieces of chocolate for each of us, otherwise David would have eaten another bar of chocolate meant for the kids when he gets in tonight.

I've suggested outdoors yoga to the class for tomorrow night since the hall is closed for the elections – so far I've had three definitely keen so it looks like that's a goer. I might as well work when I still can! Our little baby is kicking about a fair bit today, so I guess while it's being active I should be resting more.

Wednesday 2nd May

Robbie and I had a long walk in the park this morning while he was on his scooter – he took a bad bump to his head but soon got over it. This afternoon I started the new client from yesterday and she loved it… weather has been sunny and milder so this was great. I've been so excited all day about my outdoors yoga tonight!

I had another session late afternoon, I was on my bike for half the session and then doing weights for the other half. What a great day. There were eight in the jogging group tonight, one of my faster runners came along and really enjoyed it, so it worked really well. Everyone ran a fair bit faster… my heart rate was up about 160bpm which is higher than normal however I was still able to hold a conversation and it wasn't for long periods of time (we were doing 15 mins, five mins and 15 mins tempo paces with five mins walking recovery). I also had eight yoga students for my outdoor yoga which I was delighted with. In true Scotland style, the midges were out and the kids were at the nearby park later than normal too, but everyone seemed to enjoy the outdoor experience. I had my bare feet on the grass and by the end of the 45 minutes they were freezing however it was a lovely feeling, all mushy and cold after the running.

David had made a delicious chicken and pasta dish which went down very well, followed by a little crunchie chocolate. It always feels good to know I have a day off tomorrow, though I have really enjoyed training today, I know I'm going to be tired tomorrow.

Thursday 3rd May

21 weeks today and weight was eight stone 12 ¼ lbs so I was pleasantly surprised that I'm not putting on 2lbs a week as there's still a long way to go! Today, the kids were off school and nursery so it was a lovely relaxed morning. We teamed up with the kids' cousins to go to a park. The weather was fantastic today so it's been really relaxing.

I've nothing much to report today. Dinner was a big spinach and ricotta cheese pizza… Though I wasn't really feeling much like it I made a good dent in it! A client I saw yesterday cancelled tomorrow's session with a stomach bug so I really hope I don't get it as it's doing the rounds.

I've set up a "Just Giving" page to raise funds for the Eve Appeal for when I hopefully jog the women's 10K a week on Sunday. I'm just about to head off to bed at 9pm. David has been out at work all day with very little contact as usual. I feel he is so busy and when we do see each other we don't have much to say to each other before we end up bickering over something. As much as I don't mind my own company, I'm a bit worried about our relationship and the lack of communication or effort. I feel he has been involved so little in this pregnancy and that he might at least check that I'm well each day!

Friday, 4th May

Well, it's turned out to be a lazy day. I had a midwife appointment today – baby's heartbeat is strong and is growing well. We had a chat about the antenatal yoga (as this was a new midwife I hadn't met before). She was really keen and took my details and said she'd refer appropriate people on anyway. I wasn't expecting that!

Robbie went to nursery and I went a long walk in the woods, well over an hour… I just love it. I then came home knackered and went to bed. Initially, I set the alarm for 20 minutes later and then I added on another 20 minutes! Then I did a little yoga in preparation for tomorrows class and then went to pick up Jane from the neighbours.

I came back to find a missed call from my next client saying she had a bad headache and wanted to cancel today. I wasn't happy at all about this as she has cancelled three times in about three weeks. Also, it was just with over an hour's notice and I could've had my regular client at this time but it was too short notice. This means I am working longer tomorrow and this has again impacted on David's work as he wouldn't have needed to come home early tonight.

My race pack came through for next weekend's 10K race and it has got me both nervous and excited. So far my Just Giving page has raised £160 as my dad and sister have given big donations. Well, I'm chilling out now and going to bed early as tomorrow I'll be working till about 1pm and then David will be going to his work.

Saturday, 5th May

What a beautiful morning, the sunshine felt pleasantly warm at 8.30am for circuits. Although only three participants, they all really appreciated it. It was the same at the antenatal yoga – only three mums-to-be! I feel really bad about charging the girls that have paid for four weeks when they aren't there, but this is what block booking is about and this is the only way I can make the business work.

My last client was a runner and though I had planned on her doing nearly five miles, she only felt like doing three miles as she was feeling a bit dizzy. My HR stayed around 160 so I really think that after this race next week I won't be doing any more running. My pelvic floor has been a bit better though, but I really do feel like the baby is stretching my abdomen now and my bump is a recognisable baby bump!

I got home about 1pm thinking my lunch might have been made, but this was just wishful thinking. I made a big chicken salad with half a bagel. David went to work today as he's not able to work all day tomorrow. The kids just wanted to play out on the street on their bikes and scooters so I was quite happy to just sit and watch them.

After housework, dinner and bath for the kids there wasn't much else going on today. I got really grumpy with the kids after Jane had a big scream and stomp of her feet for a small thing that she said Robbie had done. For some reason, this was my trigger and I felt a bit grumpy and snappy with them till bedtime. I think I'm just tired. I'm going for a lie down now before I put our dinner in the oven... David has bought a meal of convenience for tonight – pie, beans and chips! I'm OK with this now and then but I don't think I'll bother with the chips tonight.

Well, decided against it and had a fried egg and potato scone roll as I fancied that more! It was delicious. Just had a yogurt later while me and David watched 'Mission Impossible' – I'd never seen it.

Sunday, 6th May

David went off to work early and I got the kids ready and went to mass – I feel I should make the effort every now and then as David hasn't got the time these days. Robbie thought it was great fun to drop a felt coin thing down my ever expanding cleavage! He found it even more hilarious as I tried to persuade him not to do it – he'd then lift my top up from the bottom to retrieve it and do it again!

After this we did a few arts and crafts things for me to take to my niece's birthday party.

I've only visited their new home once before and without David's sat nav I managed to get a bit lost (no surprise really!). I got a bit short with Jane as she kept saying "Mummy have you gone the wrong way again" and "When WILL we be getting there!" Well, I found it by chance – I must have a better internal navigation system than I thought! We had a great time at the party. On the way home, I managed to take the wrong slip road and so went the wrong way again... So this was Jane's cue to suggest I was going the wrong way! Well, I couldn't even admit it this time. I just said, 'Jane you are five years old and you do not know the way… this is the right way!' End of. Except, she knew she was right! Shameless of me, I know. Meanwhile, David had had someone to one time with Robbie, as no boys were invited to party. Turns out they watched football on the telly, visited his parents and then played a bit of footie.

David made a fantastic dinner of fillet steak and potato chips and vegetables with a creamy sauce – it was amazing and I was starving for it! I put a picture on Facebook, half expecting to get messages of shock from clients, instead they seemed to "like" the fact I was eating all this! Also, heard today that my sister-in-law had said it was nice to be seeing me with a bit of a tummy. Ah well, I do my best to please everyone!

Monday 7th May

Well, I got up this morning and thought about the day ahead – having the kids till after 3pm and then work until I'd get home at 10pm. I'd been up a few times through the night with the kids – not for long but still a broken sleep. On the basis that I would be running with the two middle clients, I decided it best to cancel the last session (a yoga session) as I'd need to eat or I'd be too tired to do a good session. Felt bad about this however I just need to look after myself too.

I took Jane and Robbie in to Glasgow – on a mission to get a shock absorber bra and some new socks for the race. Well it was some challenge, being in a tiny changing room with a "cowboy" swing door and two children, while changing into lots of different bras. Meanwhile the kids are either trying to escape and run around the store at top speed, or wanting to talk to the baby and stroke my tummy… at the same time as the shop assistant adjusting the bra. I managed to put one on inside out and not realise till the assistant told me.

Well, we had a fairly peaceful day the rest of the afternoon, and since the weather was poor outside we just stayed in. I went to work at 3.30pm – I was on my bike with the first client doing some intervals and then standing under a leafy tree doing some resistance work! The next two clients are running the 10K on Sunday too, so were wanting to do their longer runs – so did 4.5 miles with first one in the rain and 5 miles with next one. Both averaged out at about 13min/miles and I felt totally fine, apart from my bladder after the first hour. That was painful. My heart rate was good today… Much lower about 135bpm – 150bpm, so I'm reassured that if I get enough rest on the Saturday I should be fine. My sponsorship for The Eve Appeal is doing great too at £260, so I'm very chuffed about that.

I came home, glad I wasn't working later, and had two small salmon steaks with broccoli and bread. I also had a hot milky drink with some muesli added and then some toast and jam as I felt so hungry. It's now past 11pm and I really need to go to bed. I feel my legs are a bit heavy now so I turned my shower onto cold at the end.

Tuesday, 8th May

Well, another tired start to the day after yesterday's work. Still, I managed to wash my car after doing the school run and before meeting with friends at 10am. We went to a soft play for most of the morning and this was easy… Robbie and pals are at a great age for needing very little supervision! Had a great decaf cappuccino. Then it was the usual routine for Robbie – lunch and nursery. I had one client and for the first time this year during a session it was torrential rain. It had eased off a little as we stood under trees doing the weights session! Although, it dried up for the second half, the client didn't feel much like continuing and this was frustrating as it was only half payment. We both went a walk around the park – nice and bright weather for that!

I shouldn't complain as I was grateful to be home just for a little while before going back out to get Jane and Robbie from school. Homework was done quickly and without much fuss, so the reward chart of smiling faces seemed to be working today.

I made a lovely dinner for us – the kids had a tomato and chilli sauce with chicken, vegetables and brown rice and I had a korma sauce I'd been wanting for a while (but knew David and kids weren't going to entertain). It was nice to have something different.

My tiredness really started to take over after teatime though and it's a shame for the kids, but I do have less patience with them. I had bought a double decker chocolate bar in the shop this afternoon as an impulse buy, and already had started to nibble on a dairy milk in the cupboard! After the kids were in bed, I ate my chocolate and did a little bit of computer work. I did manage to get on my yoga mat which was a plus, as I was having doubts I would even do this. So, my session for tomorrow's class is planned and I've run through it. I've to prepare a half hour yoga class for Jane's P1 classes next week – it's their school sports week. I think I might be more nervous about this than teaching adults! Jane is very excited and I hope to start doing a lot of practise with her in the coming week and she can hopefully do this with me.

Wednesday, 9th May

It wasn't a good start to the day. David, being tired, just wanted to lie in bed this morning. I'm tired too though having been woken up with Jane during the night (she said she had a bad dream). The kids were not getting ready and emptied clothes from Robbie's drawers all over the floor. It took them an hour to get ready and I was so cross with them, but I think I was even more cross with David! If this is the help I get when he's around to get the two kids ready, I don't know what to expect when the new baby arrives since I'll need to be feeding the baby etc at the start. So, as I said, not a good start to the day.

Spent all morning in the house with Robbie – getting through the ironing and some PT work. I went for a walk, (just under the hour for about three miles) in the woods after taking Robbie to nursery, but I just felt so tired. Came home and went straight to bed for about an hour – my head was sore and I actually feel that I'm getting hay-fever today. My eyes are red and streaming and my nose hasn't stopped running.

I picked Jane up from nursery and hoped to run through some yoga with her for Monday, but she just wanted to carry on! This could be an interesting session next week. My jogging group was really good – eight turned up so I was delighted at this, though the participants ranged from faster at 9 min/mile–14 min/mile. I got them doing a lap with one as the "leader" so that no-one could over-take and this went well. It was a challenge for them – I felt pretty OK, but it was clear I was breathless with changing the paces and I didn't push myself at all. My heart rate was fine too; It didn't really go above 150 for more than a minute and I could slow right down to the slowest runners' pace for recovery. That said, I think I will switch to the bike next week so that I can go between everyone and pace them better.

The yoga tonight was really good as there were three new students, two who just turned up and have been going to yoga for several years. They really enjoyed it which was reassuring for a novice yoga teacher like me. There were three new people I expected who didn't make it tonight so that will hopefully be six new people next week! Total tonight was 10 and this felt like a good number. Quite a few of my regulars couldn't make it at the last minute so I'm hopeful my numbers might go back up to 15 or more next week which is great. I surprised myself as to how much I was still able to do, compared with how I felt earlier in the day. I guess teaching gives you a fresh burst of energy to motivate and I do love to share my practise with everyone. I did a lot of hip openers tonight and balance postures like Eagle and Warrior III. I did a short demonstration of Bakasana (crow pose) but was extra careful as this is one I should be careful with and not work my core.

Since I've been home, I've eaten a cereal bar, some toast and a hot chocolate. Off to bed now at 10.30pm.

Thursday, 10th May

Well I'm 22 weeks now and eight stone 13 ¼lb....and hardly noticing the day that I change weeks! Robbie and I met with my close yoga friend (from Teacher Training) for a coffee. Before we'd even sat down Robbie was playing with her daughter and had thrown his bag up in the air, it landed with a crash and his antihistamine medicine bottle had shattered all over his bag and was dripping everywhere! We had a really good wee catch up but it was just too short...I Had to then get back and prepared for nursery and work.

My work was with a client, running in the rain – she was running eight miles and wanted me to do the second half with her, but she'd managed five miles already and so I only had to do three miles with her. I've been really tired today and it showed with my heart rate – it seemed to go up sky high to even 180 within minutes for even the gentlest jog at 12.5-13min/mile. Just a real sign that I was very tired and my baby just wanted to be moving around and growing today I think.

I heard sad news that a girl I went to school with has breast cancer – her three teenage daughters are running in the Race for Life and she won't even be there to support them as she'll be getting her operation and then chemotherapy. It really does put your whole life in perspective.

I made a lovely lasagne and salad for us all tonight and the kids enjoyed this – I feel stuffed like I've eaten too much however I just want to eat the skinny ginger muffin I bought out of Starbucks earlier!

I'm going to chill out tonight and get to bed very early. Jane is having a massive tantrum at the moment – she wouldn't say her prayer and was being very cheeky at bedtime. I then came downstairs and she started to throw a hissy fit about wanting to say her prayers! I'm refusing to give in and she has already lost her option of a school dinner tomorrow and her swimming lesson is also now on the line.

Friday, 11th May

Well, despite getting to my bed at 9pm last night and sleeping within minutes, I woke up feeling pretty tired (before 6am right enough as Jane was up.) Of course, she was sent back to bed but within minutes Robbie appears.

I've got a busy afternoon ahead at work and so after the school run I came home and did very little. Robbie was keen to watch the "Cars" DVD so I put it on and broke it into three parts for him. I felt really guilty doing this and I never normally let them watch a full DVD, but today was a day when I needed some rest. I'm glad I did.

I had three sessions in the afternoon and it rained off and on throughout each. Just what I need to help me through my cold! I did enjoy it though, especially seeing my beginner client getting so excited about her progress and 3lb weight loss. My last session was indoors, doing yoga, and guess what, the sun shone in beautifully throughout the session! I was really glad to get home tonight though and could barely pull myself out of the shower.

I had a lovely omelette (with three eggs), salad and salad cream… I add so much salad cream to my dinner it's almost food! I've drank 2½ glasses of water and starting to feel better… Clearly I'm not drinking enough fluids.

David is heading out now, with the car though, to meet friends in town. It's a pity he can't have a drink as he can't really abandon the car when he's got the kids in the morning.

Well, early night for me again… need my rest!

Saturday, 12th May

Saturday morning circuits and the sun was shining, hooray! Glad I didn't cancel it as there were four who turned up and it was good to be out enjoying the weather. I then did the weekly shop, without children (my yoga class was cancelled as a church fayre was on).

After lunch, David went to work and I played a bit with the kids. I cleaned out my car too while they were playing in the street with the neighbours' kids. A pretty normal day really. David came home after 7pm for dinner… I made a chicken pasta dish with a pepper/mozzarella baked bread. Lovely. I had an early night, well I suppose it was about 10pm by the time I'd watched the final of Britain's Got Talent.

Sunday, 13th May

Well, not a great sleep last night. First woken up by David coming to bed around midnight, and then I just kept waking up every few hours, having a few dreams too. I felt really uncomfortable in my back and started to prop myself up with pillows. The kids woke up around 6am and from then on I was pretty much awake. I had that feeling of being so tired I feel sicky again. So, not really the best way to start the Women's 10K in Glasgow!

I was pretty grumpy too… I wanted to make sure we were there on time and get parked but David just seems to play on this and get ready really slowly. Well, we got there on time and although the day didn't start too wet it was pretty windy and cold… Not really ideal for the kids and I felt quite bad that I'd dragged them there to support me.

It took about 15 minutes before the "blue group" I was in was allowed to start and so there was a lot of standing around, although I felt pretty warm in the crowds. I went steady the whole way… With being tired my HR was up a little higher than I'd have liked at around 160bpm. But I could've talked all the way round and it actually was lower than this in the last 2 miles. My legs felt fine the whole way and breathing rate too. It was pretty wet and miserable by the time I finished… The DJ called out my name over the tannoy! I've felt really emotional all day and didn't even feel much like smiling at the end, even when I heard my name. David had headed back to the car as it was too cold and wet for the kids.

So that's it, done! I have surprised myself as I did it in 1.06 hours and this was about 10.43 min/mile average – for 22 weeks pregnant I think that's good going!! I've raised about £540 for The Eve Appeal and this makes me so happy and proud of myself.

We dropped David off for the football – last game of the season – he was going to the game with his sister. I was getting pretty tired this afternoon with the kids – they got a bit of telly while I had a shower and lunch and then we made some carrot cake cupcakes. They tasted terrible! That's the last time I buy a packet!

As the day went on, my headache was getting worse and I took a paracetamol and had a lie down when David got home. David made us all beef burgers, potato wedges and salad for dinner – it was great. I'm feeling better now though I'm going for a really early night.

I've got a few clients booked in tomorrow and two half hour yoga sessions for Jane's class at school – it's school sports week and it's a bit of a washout now. I feel like I've not done enough preparation for this but I'm too tired to care to be honest. I'm going now to put the telly on and watch "101 Dalmations" – I'll see how long I last!

Well, not long, lasted about half an hour and went to bed.

Monday, 14th May

I woke up so loaded with the cold and phlegm, it wasn't pleasant. It's really no surprise with the amount of times I've been standing in the cold getting soaked.

Today, I had the pleasure of teaching Jane's class and the composite P1/2 class some yoga. Well what a delight… Not really! They were so excited they were very hard to control and calm down. I was pretty disappointed with the teachers who were observing the class as they sat and did their own work and didn't get too involved. I don't remember being at school and being allowed to run around wild. Well, I suppose I was getting them to be all sorts of different animals and play games and have fun too. I finished it with a visualisation lasting just a few minutes, where they were to picture a lake and all the surroundings. It did end quite peacefully. Jane was so excited to be showing off her Mum to the class and taking a few liberties like drinking my water. She later said everyone was asking, "Was that your mum?" I don't think she got all her work done today!

The rest of the day I had three more clients – I could well have just gone to bed, though a paracetamol took the edge off my cold. Two clients were outside and fortunately we were saved from the rain that had been torrential earlier today. Two of the clients had done the 10K yesterday and were looking for a good stretching session combined with core work. My muscles haven't felt heavy or different at all for doing the 10K which is really encouraging for me. My bump is definitely bigger than it was with Robbie and so I think this baby might be bigger still.

This doesn't seem to stop new potential clients stopping me during sessions and asking for PT sessions! I gave my card out to another girl, though I'm thinking this is more for when my classes continue in the future, when I'm on maternity leave.

I got in after 8pm tonight and David had made me a lovely chicken stir-fry. I followed this with a FAB ice-lolly while doing my PC updates… And then went to bed! 9.30pm, hope to get rid of this cold fast!

Tuesday, 15th May

I feel like I'm a really light sleeper these days and can't remember the last time I slept through the night. I was only up once but woke up another time I'm sure.

Robbie and I headed to park to meet friends with their scooters. It wasn't long before there was a fall so the scooters were abandoned. It was freezing too – it's May and still feels like February!

I went to the pharmacy to get my "healthy start" vitamins for during pregnancy however they are out of stock and can't seem to get a hold of them! That's not a good sign – government introduce a new scheme to ensure expectant and nursing mums get enough vitamin D and then run out.

I also went to the supermarket for bread and milk and as usual, came out with a whole lot more. Which reminds me, as I write this I've remembered my plan for tonight was to touch up the grey roots on my hair – I can't believe how grey I'm getting, and how quickly after I've just dyed my hair.

I had a client today and I was on my bike while she ran five miles – this is a great job sometimes… Weather had warmed up a bit too. The kids were fine the rest of the day, out on their scooters and bikes with friends – usual stuff. They had macaroni and I had an omelette and salad again.

I'm going to get my hair dyed now and have an early night, though I will likely wake up when David gets in later.

Wednesday, 16th May

Well, what a great little morning I had with Robbie. We went to a "musical times" session for toddlers. Robbie was so excited and loved every minute of it. I loved seeing him so confident and happy, singing along and dancing to all the songs. I will go for the next five weeks before it ends for the summer break. He even said in the car on the way home that he most liked that I was doing it with him… I suppose a lot of the time I'm doing other things in the house when he's there and also I didn't do as many of these group sessions with Robbie as I did with Jane. He's going through a fantastic phase of saying how much he loves me and it's more than making up for the difficulties I have with Jane a lot of the time.

So Robbie went to nursery and I had a client in the afternoon then went a walk (while I still can). When I came home I was really tired so I had a nap and then I did my yoga practise/ preparation for the session tonight. Only five people turned up to the jogging group and only five to the yoga! I used my bike for the jogging group tonight as I just feel I don't want to run much anymore. I heard there was a bingo night on at the school opposite where the yoga takes place, and this explained why quite a few of my students weren't there.

I've also arranged cover for my Wednesday class and my antenatal class too in the next month or so. It's good to know that I won't be totally starting from scratch when I return from maternity leave. I'm getting enquiries every day about either the yoga or personal training, which is really encouraging but I know I'll need to start turning away business.

I had a pizza when I got in from yoga and watched The Apprentice… Little pleasures of mine!

Thursday, 17th May

Well, 23 weeks today… Forgot to weigh myself. I had an easy morning to myself as Robbie went to gymnastics with his friend and his grandparents. I was getting a bit worried when he didn't get back after 11am – it was nearer 12pm. The gran said she'd taken them a walk along a nature trail after it in East Kilbride… I would've just liked a text! Robbie was starving for his lunch – he is a little bit of a creature of habit and said he'd been keen to get home.

After his nursery, I took him for his annual allergy test at the hospital. It's a year since his last major reaction to something. Well, he was so brave and easy going during all the skin prick tests. He appears to have all the same allergies – Egg, Nuts, Lentils, Peas and also Seeds and Prawns. His wee arm was all sore and inflamed and clearly itchy.

We've just to carry on with the same anti-histamine at a higher dose if he gets a reaction.

As a treat, we went to Pizza Hut – so it was another pizza for me tonight! I had a vegetarian one with goats cheese and rocket… it was alright, nothing special.

Our baby is well and truly kicking now and I can actually see the kicks through my clothes! It's an early night for me tonight.

Friday, 18th May

Well, I woke up and just felt really tired again and the cold seems to have worked its way back on me. The thought of work this afternoon was not one I was relishing, but I guess it's not for much longer. I took the kids to their walking bus this morning and it was freezing! It's the middle of May and the temperature is about 6C with a biting wind.

I spent a bit of time this morning planning this afternoon's work. I had to take both bikes to the park and so to do this without having a mad rush after nursery I just took them over this morning. It was so awkward trying to lift the heavy mountain bike that David has, but I eventually managed it. I wouldn't have dared to do these things in my first pregnancy.

My next client's this afternoon were new girls at Strathclyde Park and I was so glad to meet them, even though I might only meet them a few times. They are both trying for babies and have had various problems along the way. They were so friendly and easy to get on with that you couldn't not instantly like them. I should see them again in two weeks as one of them has booked a last minute holiday this week.

My last client was a regular that I would normally run with however I've said I'm not doing this anymore. She was happy to do yoga and weights combined for the remaining time. Before, I went to her house at 6pm I managed to quickly make a salmon steak and potato salad. This was perfect as when I got back at 7.30pm I had to drive David to a fundraising night out. I was feeling so tired and quite grumpy. When I got back, I put the kids in bed, had a FAB ice-lolly and then went to bed.

Saturday, 19th May

It's not been a brilliant day for me. I woke up still loaded with this cold. I had another night of broken sleep – mostly because of David coming in from a night out and his snoring waking me up several times. It's enough to make anyone grumpy. I left the dishes in the sink last night piled up high – this is something David does to make it look like he's tidied the kitchen. In fact, if he'd emptied the dishwasher and loaded it up again that would have been better. Well hangover or not, I was going to work and most definitely doing less housework that involved lifting and lugging things around.

My circuits class was poorly attended again, with only three clients – I did make them work pretty hard. It was cold but at least dry and the wind had settled a bit – so overall much better than last week. The antenatal yoga was fine, a few people didn't make it but my neighbour that's expecting twins came and also a girl that had been in the first block too. So there were five girls which was quite good going. The hall is always freezing though and it would be nice if we didn't have the big noisy fan heater on. One of the girls is 38 weeks pregnant and looking amazing with her neat little bump.

I came home and it looked like David had just got up and the kids had been in front of the telly for a while. I said to David I was going to be doing less about the house and not coming in from work to do all the tidying up again. He started saying I was snapping at him and that everyone was getting on fine. I said I was simply making it known that I needed some rest today. I've had a tough week with the cold and working in this weather, and yes, I'm allowed to feel exhausted anyway, because I am pregnant! He said, 'You will go off and run a 10K and if you want to be less tired then maybe you ought not to have done this.' He really knows how to make my blood boil. I was very upset today for hours on end. I feel like this has been building up… I notice this as I've been making little comments to my clients about David and that's when I realise I'm overflowing with a bit of resentment. As I said to David today, all I'm wanting is a bit more gratitude, nothing more. He said, 'This is what life is like.' And that, 'Yes, you do have to keep a clean house too.' I said I feel that for all I do with trying to keep working in a physical job, maintain the house and run around with the kids school/nursery runs that all I get when he is around is criticism about doing more. The other day, he'd suggested that I could be doing the supermarket weekly shop one of the mornings of the week when I've got Robbie! I explained that not only do I do a lot of housework in the mornings already and make sure Robbie gets plenty stimulation out-with the house (David had requested a few months ago, when I was feeling ropey in my first trimester, that I should take Robbie swimming or to gymnastics weekly), but I'm also preparing for my own work! He seems to think I'm a lady of leisure.

So today I stayed in while David went out to play with the kids and then went to park to play football – he sent Jane in to ask if I wanted to come but I was so teary and knackered that I said no. Instead, I just got on with some paperwork that needed doing.

David doesn't actually seem to know how to say sorry, he just thinks that after a few hours and a bit of space, I will be happy and smiling again. He arrives back home and does the usual big Cheshire smiling cat thing that actually makes me annoyed again. If he could take the hint and just say "Sorry, I do appreciate all you do", then that would be enough.

He went back out to do the weekly shop which was fine. I made pasta for me and the kids. David came home with a pregnancy magazine, I guess as a way of saying sorry and a piece of carrot cake I'd requested. It did break the ice this time, but I'm still feeling emotionally drained today.

The Champions League final has been on the telly all night… It's now 9.30pm and I think I should just go to bed.

Sunday, 20th May

David let me lie in bed till about 8am this morning, I went back to bed with my breakfast too which was nice. I've had a totally chilled out day with the kids – no hurry in the world and plenty time outdoors in the sunshine. Yes… The sunshine! It's been warmer and we even had a picnic at Kelvingrove Park where we met a friend. The kids had a great time hiding in the bushes, playing on their scooters and at the park. They've been so well behaved too. Robbie even conquered his fear of going down big enclosed helter skelter slides… He was so excited once he had done it and Jane was so helpful with him.

We spent the rest of the afternoon at home in the garden and drawing pictures, while I read a baby magazine. I've now just been working away with emails and updates and have a small ironing to do for the school clothes tomorrow.

Monday, 21st May

It's now Tuesday night and I'm really struggling to remember what I did yesterday!

I had a chat with one of the girls who started training last week as her health questionnaire didn't quite add up. It never ceases to amaze me how some people are such survivors of life's difficulties and others sink at the first signs of change or challenge. This girl has had so much loss over the years it's so admirable and inspiring that she can be so upbeat and positive about life. She'd had an ectopic pregnancy in January this year. She has a two-year-old girl, however before her she lost a baby in the neonatal unit. She also lost her sister in a car crash a number of years ago. I really admire how strong some people are and it humbles me to have met her.

It was also a beautiful sunny warm day and I had a last-minute cancellation at lunchtime which was disappointing, given the weather. I made the most of it though and went a long walk for about an hour through the woods. I came home and prepared my sessions for the evening – three more sessions, starting at 5.30pm.

The first session was a weights circuit in Glasgow – that was fine though the midges were a nuisance. For the next session I did a little bit of running with the client – only about three-four minutes and to be honest, it felt really uncomfortable where our baby was sitting. I really do think it's time to totally stop the running.

My last session was doing yoga in my clients' home, and this is even really starting to become a bit uncomfortable now… Given that the session starts at 8.30pm. I came home and had a banana and a hot milky drink.

Should have got to bed earlier but it was after 11pm before I was in bed.

Tuesday, 22nd May

Well, I think today might be remembered for the way I've suddenly felt like a beach whale and everyone has been commenting on how much bigger I have got. As David said, I've been wearing a top that has done me no favours in that department and from the minute I put it on, I knew it was going to make me look big. It does get a bit annoying though to have people comment on my size so much.

I got on with housework this morning while Robbie played with a friend. The weather was beautiful and hot again today and I've scoffed two ice-lollies! Much needed. David also bought me a curly wurly for after my dinner tonight so that went down not too badly! I am having a fair amount of sweets though.

I had a running client today and I was on my bike, however for the first time I even felt a little uncomfortable on my bike. Also, my back has been achy and feeling pretty weak. I felt really nauseous by early evening time and had to have a nap once the kids were in their beds. I hope this is just the weather and not a sign of things to come.

Jane and Robbie were pretty good after school and nursery. They've been so lovely talking to the baby. Unbe-known to them, Robbie talks to my bellybutton and refers to "He" and Jane does the same and refers to "She"! It's so funny.

David came home at 7.30pm tonight which has been nice. We sat and had dinner together but I know he's feeling anxious about his work and the difficulty in getting someone to come and work with him.

I'm going to watch a murder/mystery drama on telly now as a break from anything else and then head to bed.

Wednesday, 23rd May

What a gorgeous day it's been today; washing was hung out first thing and it felt like mid-afternoon on a hot summers day, and only at 8am. Temperatures got to about 25C and it was hot, hot, hot! I had a pretty relaxing day today – just had wee Robbie at the park this morning before taking him to the musical times session. I love this and Robbie is so animated and full of life and fun – he has such a brilliant easy going nature and makes me laugh and smile so much.

We had our lunch out the back garden again and then I went a walk at the park while he was in nursery. I had a rest and a little time for meditation while sitting on a bench – unusual for me to stop mid walking but it was hot and I had blisters too!

I've drank loads of water today and felt much better today than yesterday despite it being hotter. I cancelled my jogging group tonight as only 1 could make it and it's just not worth my while doing it at this stage for one person. Only four students turned up at yoga tonight, and given the weather I even doubted if anyone was going to turn up. I really enjoyed the session, despite feeling really hot, I am still managing quite a lot of poses like the revolved triangle and fish pose still feels pretty good. I did a practise run out the back garden this afternoon, and this was just bliss.

I sat down tonight to some pizza and salad and David had bought me a Callipo ice-lolly from the tally van! I should be in my bed now as it's nearly 11pm, however, I've checked my emails from my website and have another enquiry to follow up. This person is keen to just get started and has been referred through one of my antenatal students, so I'll see how much I can help. Bed calling, little baby kicking!

Thursday, 24th May

Well I'm 24 weeks today and I remembered to weigh myself and to my shock I really am putting on plenty pounds! I was nine stone 3lb – 4lbs heavier than two weeks ago… I really hope I don't put on 2lb a week as I'm already starting to feel pretty uncomfortable.

It's been a mega heat wave again today. I didn't do much with Robbie this morning – just to the supermarket to buy more water and ice-lollies! It's almost been too hot for me again. I washed the car and played a new catch/ball game with Robbie.

I had another walk of about an hour at the park through the woods again. Feeling like it's a slog already and finding it hard in my head to consider myself as a PT when I can't even do what I'm asking clients to do. But I also know I must carry on for as long as possible as it's going to be a long time going in if I stop now.

The kids had lots of fun after school playing in the garden and dancing in the house. I made a prawn stir-fry with noodles – Robbie had the same minus the prawns! I feel so full up and my stomach actually feels really stretched and uncomfortable. I really didn't feel this way with Jane or Robbie and am preparing myself to really grow and grow for a while. This doesn't really please me, I'd rather have a petite little bump!

It doesn't help that I've just munched my way through a packet of maltesers!

Going to bed soon, as feeling tired and need to catch up on sleep; last night was too late and tomorrow is a busy afternoon.

Friday, 25th May

Another week nearly over, can't believe it's the end of May and it felt like just yesterday I took Jane to her cousins birthday party at the beginning of the month.

This morning I cleaned my outdoor groundsheets for work and played games in the garden with Robbie.

I had a full afternoon (three clients) at the park from 1.15 onwards – mostly all weights work with a tiny bit of running with a fairly new client (3 x 3min). This is about as much running as I plan to do now. I really feel big for this stage of pregnancy and everyone is telling me this too. I'm getting a bit weary of it… It is my third pregnancy and I'm meant to put on weight!

My last client, booked for 6pm, cancelled this morning however it wasn't enough time to fill the space with the two people that normally look for this session. It did however mean that I could take Jane to her swimming lesson and I had a swim too (50 lengths). David made chicken fajitas for dinner, of which I had four… This is actually normal for me but now it is feeling a bit greedy, and my exercise levels are indeed going down. I'm contemplating an early night with a hot chocolate now! I've been doing more research on YouTube for my antenatal yoga classes as I like to keep them varied and fresh.

Saturday, 26th May

I had a really good morning at work – there may only have been three at circuits this morning but I got them working really hard doing shuttle runs, hopping, backward lunges, burpees and lots of core work. Then I had my antenatal yoga class and there were six attended – this was a good class and I enjoyed it. After this, I had a new PT client at the park – weather has still been glorious too. She is about a size 20 and desperate for a lifestyle change. I've given her short term goals for this week that she agreed on; also to do the "wheel of life" exercise to try and get a better, healthier balance and to focus on the priorities in her life.

Once I came home, I got changed and ready for David's family coming round for a BBQ – we all had a lovely afternoon, eating and drinking. I had plenty prawn kebabs and some chicken salad for dinner. David made everyone fillet steak but I wasn't overly keen to have much meat… Maybe it was the amount of crisps I'd already eaten. The kids had a ball with the paddling pool out.

By the time everyone left and the kids were in bed, it was after 8.30pm. There wasn't much left of me by then… I suddenly felt really tired and the left side of the middle of my back has been getting sore later on every day. Also, I've started to get the "jumpy legs" or "restless legs" syndrome again – I had this with Jane and it's so annoying as you just feel restless like you want to fidget your legs all the time. I was in bed reading the paper by 10pm.

Sunday, 27th May

We've had a really lazy day today – we didn't go anywhere, just enjoyed the sun in the back garden and then up at the neighbours' house. I spent most of the morning getting washings done and tidying up from yesterday.

I made us all a baked potato with chicken and salad for dinner and once again have had two ice-lollies today. My back is sore again… Same place, and I just feel like going to bed, even though it's only 8pm. I'm not feeling up to doing any yoga though it would probably help my back. David has been at work all day, such a shame as it's been really, really hot again, in fact so hot I've preferred to sit in the shade most of the day.

Monday, 28th May

I didn't have a great night's sleep last night. Jane was in a few times from having a nightmare. She said a wicked witch was trying to take her and Robbie away, wee soul! Then I was awake a few times just with the daylight and I think Robbie was in quite early, before 6am.

The day started off really hot again and then got gradually cooler and a bit windy, but that was a welcome relief. I really have stopped running now with clients and my bump certainly feels like it's getting a bit awkward for me in certain positions. I had two clients today in the sunshine and then came home; had an ice-lolly and a wee nap before heading back out for the last two sessions. One was in the house as the little park at the end of the street was too busy, and the other was my yoga client. She suggested we do the yoga in the back garden which was just divine. One of my clients said I now looked "massive" – why is it people think that this is going to be a welcome comment for anyone even if they are pregnant? I have just been getting used to the fact that in this job everyone feels they have to pass some remark about how big I am getting and how surprised they are to see my bump.

Came home and had a lovely salmon and vegetable cous cous dinner, followed by quite a few crisps. Going to bed now as I'm getting tired and 10pm is fast approaching. Baby is kicking away though the kicks are pretty light and I'm starting to maybe change my tune about the baby being a boy!

Tuesday, 29th May

We spent the morning round at my neighbours. The kids were so well behaved and we really could have a proper adult chat. That's all to change again so soon!

I had a client after dropping off Robbie – I was on the bike, and still managing to lift this on and off the car rack. I am however starting to notice that the bump is slightly getting in the way of being comfortable while on the bike and think this will need to stop in a few weeks. I've also felt like I've had hay-fever today – I've been sneezing lots and my eyes and nose have been streaming, and really sensitive when outside.

I had an easy-going afternoon with the kids after school time, and they were out on their scooters and bikes a lot before bedtime. Today it was still pretty mild (17 C) but overcast… Which has been a blessing!

I made pasta in a tomato and bacon sauce tonight for us all and once the kids were in bed had a milky decaf coffee and a wispa. Also today I've had one of David's mini thornton millionaire shortcakes and a FAB ice lolly. My lunch was a cheese and banana toastie and then yogurt. I've had lots of fruit today – pink grapefruit, banana, cherries, raspberries and an apple. I'd say that's a pretty balanced diet.

Wednesday, 30th May

Here I am again, on a Thursday and trying to remember what I did on a Wednesday! Apart from taking Robbie to his wee musical times session the morning was pretty much the same stuff with my great buddy boy.

I had two clients at work this afternoon doing weights/ conditioning sessions and then the jogging group and yoga. Since six people cancelled the jogging group in the 20 minutes before it started, I can't really call it a group, with one person there. I was on my bike and from lifting that at least four times on and off the car I really wasn't too happy about the last minute cancellations. I'm trying to fill that slot with a PT session instead as it's not worth my while if people aren't able to make it.

At least yoga was better attended with 10 people there – we did mostly forward and back bending for a change.

I came home and didn't really eat any more than toast – just wasn't feeling like it.

Thursday, 31st May

Well, 25 weeks today… Another week has rolled on by. My weight is nine stone 3lbs so glad it's not gone up another 2lbs from last week! My tummy is feeling really stretched and my breasts are so swollen and pretty uncomfortable. I've clearly not got very good posture as my back is sore by the end of the day… Maybe my chest is bigger than the last time too.

Robbie and I went swimming this morning – he's doing great, really trying to swim unaided. After doing a few wee odd jobs and some supermarket stuff, I dropped Robbie off at nursery. I had a rare wee hour or so to myself before I had to go to Robbie's Jubilee party at the nursery. I'd bought a magazine and enjoyed a wee milky decaf coffee and a chocolate biscuit before having a 15 minute nap. Robbie's Jubilee party was such a laugh – all the groups had made things for the

Jubilee and were showcasing them and then getting awards, it was hilarious. Robbie loved it.

I sneaked out of the party to pick up Jane from school – this being their last day till next Wednesday because of the Jubilee holidays.

The rest of the day we just played outdoors on bikes and scooters and then indoors doing gluing and glittering crowns. I had a full pizza – a roasted vegetable and pesto one, with salad! I've also had a glass of coke as I had a wee notion, and then another chocolate biscuit. Maybe not quite what you'd expect for the diet of a personal trainer!

I've really noticed this last week that I'm getting back pain most evenings, heartburn from lunchtime onwards and jumpy restless legs in the evening too.

Friday, 1st June

The kids are off school and nursery for a holiday so my Mum came over to watch them while I went to work. My first client was in their house doing yoga, the next client was at the park doing a combination of weights and running (I was on the bike). By then, the day had really heated up… My Mum had brought the kids to the park and I could hear them shouting "Mummy" at the top of their voices during my last session.

I had a little hour at home to rest and eat and then my last client was at Springburn Park doing weights, boxing and some jogging. I decided to do some jogging with this client as it was slow enough for me – it was 2 x 10 mins roughly and I felt fine… I didn't however have my HR monitor on, but I could talk easily throughout the run, despite the heat. I really enjoyed running again and felt like I'd been missing it already!

We all ate a pre-packed ready meal of cannelloni for dinner – it was sweet potato, spinach and goats cheese, together with salad and crisps, it was lovely.

Well, I'm heading off for a bath now; I feel like I need a good soak and some baby time. I've had a little milky way and think I'll now have a hot chocolate in the bath (with some marshmallows thrown in too!).

For tomorrow's circuits I have a list of about eight people who have said they are coming – this will be interesting to see!

Saturday, 2nd June

Well no great surprises, though disappointed! Only three for circuits and two for yoga this week! It feels hardly worth carrying on the circuits and I probably will stop at the end of June. Also, the church hall for yoga was decked in Diamond Jubilee celebrations – all tables out and tea waiting to be served! The event didn't start till 2pm however they had decided to be super organised. Not much space for a yoga class but then only two turned up!

When I got home, I had a wee lie down before the crew came back from Jane's gymnastics and shopping trip. We all had lunch together and then a bit of play in the back garden. Then, I did some housework/ ironing while David tidied out the garage and the kids played out the front. It was good we all spent some time together later – a trip to the dump and to B&Q! We all had dinner together too; I made a chicken and pasta dish. I don't know what's up with me today though, just not had my usual appetite… I didn't enjoy my dinner one bit and so where I normally go back and have a second helping I just didn't bother.

I booked a holiday online for us all to go to St Andrews in July… I'm really happy we've something organised. It's for a week and David will come for three-four days. It's a cottage with a sea view and near the beach. It's only really a month away so I should still be really active and mobile.

Me and David sat watching a film tonight which was really nice. Because of my jumpy restless legs, I had to sit with my legs up against the chair and my back propped up so I wasn't lying flat. We only watched the first half and then went to bed.

Sunday, 3rd June

Well, a wee day to myself with the kids… I didn't rush the morning and headed out to Pollock park by about 11. I had a lovely walk with the kids on their scooters and then a picnic on a bench. It was fresh and a bit chilly and the rain didn't look far away so we then went to "sporty kids" a soft play. The kids love this place and I got some time to sit and read my magazine. I had a decaf cappuccino and we all shared a piece of carrot cake… It was delicious, I'll need to remember it's good here!

Once we came home, I had a bit of a kick-off from Jane – stomping her feet about absolutely everything and being cheeky and difficult. She and Robbie managed to break one of the sideboard doors – it's not just off its hinge, the actual wood is burst! David is going to be furious as I really don't see it being able to be fixed. Jane spent a bit of time in her room to calm down as she was shouting at Robbie and blaming him, and what with all her stomping I'd had enough! They both had another wee play outside on their scooters while I made a roast duck for dinner.

I pulled the duck out to try and use some of the fat on the potatoes and carrots and the fat exploded in my face and hands – quickly got a dishcloth to my face and think I'll only have a few wee burns on my hands and one on my face if I'm lucky. I'm dreading bringing it out the oven again…

Well, I didn't get burnt again, however, the rest of the night didn't go too well as David arrived home to find the broken sideboard door. Let's say he was pretty cross and shouted so loud at the kids at dinner time, I had to leave the table. I was so angry with his outburst as I'd already given the kids into trouble and he just upset everyone. At the end of the day, it's just a sideboard and it was an accident. No surprise then that David ate his dinner and then left for work again, and came in very late. I was raging as this was so unfair on the kids. In a fury, I sent a text saying pretty much this and expecting an apology. Well, I haven't had one yet and I'm writing this on Monday night!

Monday, 4th June

Holiday Monday today, so no school or nursery. I took the kids out to Bothwell Castle for an explore through the castle and forest grounds, then we played a few ball games. Robbies favourite was "fetch" – I was to be the dog and pant every time he threw the ball for me to fetch! What a laugh.

Then we went to Strathclyde Park on the bikes – Jane is doing brilliant cycling without any stabilisers and weaving in and out of people. We had a picnic and spent some time at the play-park. When we got home, I was shattered and let them watch some telly to chill out while I had a power nap before getting ready for work.

I only had two clients today, but even the thought of that made me feel so tired. My first client was a runner so I was on my bike for the hour. The next client was boxing and doing a weights circuit, and then after this I had a half hour on the bike to myself. I just felt like I needed a bit of my own time… Still feeling pretty sad about David and I not getting on but I really don't want to back down till he says sorry. He did try before I went to work with a "Can we be friends?" but I said he really ought to say sorry.

When I came home, I sent a message to all the jogging group to say that it won't be on any more so that I can take time on maternity leave – I was just getting so scunnered that people weren't coming when they said they would, and it's more than my energy is worth at this time of night. A few more weeks and Angie will be taking over my yoga class too.

The Queens Jubilee concert was on telly tonight so I watched a bit of this with a big bowl of cereal and a toasted roll and then went to bed. Sleeping by 9.30pm.

Tuesday, 5th June

It's another holiday today because of the Queens Jubilee and so we went swimming. I really see a big difference with Jane and her swimming – she was doing well giving it her best shot. Robbie was trying too and they all seemed to have a good time. I've just been doing washings, ironings and tidying up this afternoon.

We had a good afternoon – the kids all got on great. I made baked tatties for dinner and egg mayonnaise and beans for me.

I also managed some yoga practise tonight though it really made my heartburn worse being inverted in pyramid or down-dog poses. I plan to do Salute to the Moon tomorrow night in the class as we've not done it in a while.

Wednesday, 6th June

Well surprise, surprise, the rain came on this morning and Jane's school sports day was cancelled… Again! I'm more disappointed by this than anything else to do with her schoolwork as I know how much she loves running around!

Instead, I took Robbie to the Musical Times session.

I was meant to have two clients this afternoon – for the first we did a weights session under the trees in the warmish rain! The next one rearranged her time twice such that I had already made plans for picking up the kids. I've now got her booked in for tomorrow.

I had my bike on the car and as there was only meant to be 45 minutes between sessions I just decided to go a walk… Only to get back to the car and find the client had wanted to change time again as stuck in a meeting. So, I decided to go around the park on my bike this time – though I really am starting to feel like my bump is getting in the way of the cycling when my knees come up.

I picked up the kids and did all the usual stuff. When David came in I did a bit of preparation for yoga tonight… It was quite nice to not be rushing to the jogging group and sitting having dinner with the kids. Jane and I had lovely salmon and vegetables.

Yoga went well – there were nine students who turned up – different people from last week but the numbers are at least averaging out. I added in the shoulder-stand and just talked them all through it. This seemed to go OK.

Thursday, 7th June

Today I am 26 weeks… I can't believe how fast the weeks are going by. I weighed myself and am nine stone 3.5lbs, so happy I'm not piling the weight on, though my bump is feeling very big! David and I are still not saying a word to each other… Both very stubborn I guess; I'd rather make a point that it's not ok to shout and be so angry with the kids and have everyone upset. He really should say sorry. I know he's working really hard, but so is everyone.

It really pisses me off that he turns his working long hours into being for my benefits. He said he's working all the hours so that there is no pressure on me to work when I go on maternity leave. I don't actually see any pressure on me to work and only weeks ago he was saying I should finish up whenever I felt like it if I was too tired to work. Now it's all for my benefit. Well, hello, but I thought he'd known all along that when he set up the business he'd be working all the hours anyway to get it established… Whether there was a baby on the way or not! OK, rant over.

I had a lovely wee morning with Robbie at the shops… Bought birthday cards and a present for a niece and then decided once again to treat the kids with a new toy out of ASDA – they only cost £5 each but I felt they deserved it.

I had my client today that was rearranged from yesterday and was lucky that it managed to stay dry. I still lugged the bike and rack on the car in case it rained and she wanted a running session, but we did weights for the hour.

I picked the kids up from school and had invited Jane's friend to stay for dinner. I made spaghetti bolognaise from scratch so was delighted when they ate every last bit of it. It was pretty good, though the spaghetti stuck together – probably because I got cheap stuff out of Poundland today!

I'm planning on a relaxing night tonight – my back is pretty sore with all the housework I've been doing and time on my feet, so I may even have a bath. I've a piece of carrot cake waiting for me too out of BOOTS so I'm sure I'll have that later!

Friday, 8th June

The Jubilee celebration for Jane's school was going on today, so she was all dressed up in a party dress. The celebration was a school buffet of sausage rolls and sandwiches and ice-cream. Peer pressure meant she was having a school lunch again, though I'd given her money on Wednesday thinking they'd have had the celebrations then. Maybe I'm tight with money, but £1.85 for a kids' lunch seems a bit much for me and I don't think sausage roll and beans and cake is really much of a healthy option. I think she gets more TV at school than at home too; she was telling me today she saw some Scooby doo and Aladdin!

Well that's a moan again about the school and there was more to come later today! But back to the morning – just usual fun daily stuff with Robbie… the post office and banking. He went to nursery and I had a client doing weights work – it was dry for the first half and then unfortunately the rain couldn't hold back anymore. I then decided to go a walk in the rain… with my brolly, just for some me time. I really enjoyed it and even tried a wee jog for five minutes but that was about all I felt like… but it made me feel a bit more like me again.

My next client was indoors doing yoga so this was just lovely. I had a cancellation with one client as she had a got a ticket to the see the Olympic torch in George Square today. It's great seeing so much interest in the torch travelling across the country.

After Jane's swimming class we all had a quick pizza dinner. I had some nice dark chocolate, infused with oranges as a dessert!

Well, the other gripe about the school has been the letter telling us that Jane is in the composite class for next year. Ah well, I think I saw it coming but I'm still pretty disappointed as I don't like the idea of a mixed level class and hope it's not a sign that she will be in composite classes throughout school.

Saturday, 9th June

I had a great morning at work. Weather was surprisingly pleasant and warm. I had four girls for circuits and I enjoyed working them hard! Then I had five for my antenatal yoga class – think I enjoyed this class more than any of the others. The hall was warmer from the start and the sun was coming in. I changed my music and I had the girls facing the windows and at the brighter end of the room. I think it all made a difference! Last of all, I had a client who has been struggling with motivation – I think I've got her set up for the week now… She is a classic example of someone that believes "Well, that's just me, and that's what I've always done". So hopefully, we've started to address the negative self-talk.

I came home and we all made more of an effort to get on… I guess that's the war over for me and David – it lasted nearly a whole week which is unheard of. There was still no apology but it had gone on long enough. We all went out on our bikes for a little while this afternoon – just up the street, but it was really nice. It's a pity that's the first we've done it as in a few weeks' time I won't be getting on a bike!

Just a relaxing afternoon and plenty chat in the evening between David and I which was really good. He made a nice wee fillet steak (it was tiny) and I followed this with some of his galaxy chocolate!

My dad phoned tonight and we also had a good catch up – his wife is pretty unwell and his life revolves around caring for her. It's mostly sympathy for my dad that I have as he doesn't seem to have much of an exciting time either, and he certainly doesn't see much of the rest of the family. Think I've seen him once this year which I find really sad.

David and I had a later night than we both imagined but we had a week to catch up on!

Sunday, 10th June

David was up at the crack of dawn and Jane was awake and through for a cuddle at 6.15am! Way too early and I feel I have suffered for it pretty much all day.

I took the kids swimming with their friends and they all had a great time. I see such a difference in the kids' confidence now and Jane is showing off her swimming skills to everyone. We came home and had a lovely toastie for lunch with crisps… Only thing is I got totally in a trance while eating the crisps out the bag that I nearly ate the whole lot (it was a big family bag!) After this and a hot chocolate, it really was time for a lie down! So the kids got some telly time and I had a sleep of about 30 minutes!

I needed that though as I then was out in Glasgow meeting my sister and brother-in-law for dinner in Princes Square before we all went to see my mum sing in her choir at St Andrews Cathedral. It was really good and I'm proud that she has found something that she enjoys and has a good social life. It was even better to see my sister a bit happier and also asking questions about my pregnancy. I was a bit embarrassed at first and still felt a little uncomfortable talking about it however it was a good sign. When I got home after 9.30pm tonight I had some really sore cramps, but I think this was more a sign of wind than anything else! In bed for 10.30pm.

Monday, 11th June

Well a busy wee day ahead for me. David was up well before 6am and gone to work. The morning routine with the kids alone can be quite exhausting especially when I get some resistance about getting ready. I didn't do a great deal with Robbie this morning, but instead did a fair bit of housework – washings and ironings.

I had a client after dropping Robbie off at nursery – she was so lovely and gave me a gift for the baby and a voucher too. So, so generous and it's great that I have a job where you get on with everyone. I do feel a bit sad though that I'm not going to see a lot of my clients as they are like friends and they are my social life!

I had a wee afternoon nap and then had three clients back to back – one in Glasgow, doing weights and conditioning in her flat, the next one at the local park doing a circuit/weights session and then my last client at 8.30pm – yoga in her house. I decided that tonight would be the last night of doing the yoga at this time as I'm just so tired. Also I was suffering from the heartburn pretty badly today. I don't think I should be eating tomatoes… Just like Robbie has told me – babies don't like tomatoes!! The voice of reason!

I had some porridge of all things, before going to bed about 10.30pm.

Tuesday, 12th June

David was up super early again today. If ever there was a day when I started to feel heavily pregnant it was today! I actually feel like I'm the size I was when I was full term with Robbie! HELP!

I went round the park with Robbie on his scooter and then my neighbour came in for a chat. There's a lot of talk at the moment about the composite class and the reasons why. I've still to have a chat with the school which I reckon I should do, but I still wish Jane wasn't in the composite class.

I had a lovely wee hour to myself today… Having no clients to rush to was nice. I went a walk but felt pretty tired and warm and decided to make it a short walk instead and get an ice-lolly and a paper. Then I had a nap before picking up the kids. Jane had a belter of a tantrum about doing her homework and so there was no outside play or telly for them tonight. The night did seem to go in pretty quickly though. The kids had a baked potato and I had omelette, tuna and beans. I've since had some strawberries and now wondering what else to eat. This is what most of my clients find difficult… Trying to curb the boredom eating in the evening. I don't really need anything else to eat so I'll see if I can manage – unless I get hungry!

Well, I managed not to eat anything else so that's all good!

Wednesday, 13th June

I've had a lovely day today as my dad was visiting. We had a smashing time with Robbie as we took him to his Musical Steps class and dad got the chance to sing, play and dance along. I had another enquiry from a pregnant Mum about my yoga class which was good. If I can keep a healthy number of mums coming to this class on a Saturday that will make it feel more worthwhile.

My dad then took us for a good lunch at the log cabin – I had a cheese, tomato and pesto panini.

It's been so good to see how happy Dad is around Robbie (Jane was at school) and he kept saying he wished he lived nearer that he could just pop in and see them more often. He got to see Robbie's nursery and again how settled he is in there. Robbie had a graduation afternoon, which I didn't go to as it's not his real graduation from nursery… Just to move him into his pre-school year. He made a hat for the occasion and he was given a certificate when they called his name out. I think it's a bit over the top that nurseries do any graduation at all, but we'll make a big deal of it next year just like we did with Jane.

I picked the kids up later after doing some yoga practise and preparation for my class later. My client at 5.30pm cancelled 20 minutes before her session – this is pretty frustrating and I feel guilty taking money but my business will be stopping shortly and she is cancelling for her own work reasons which I can't keep accommodating.

Fiona came to take part in the class as she will be taking it over as of next week. I really feel like the timing has been perfect as I'm getting tired and uncomfortable by the evening time. I'm starting to find it more difficult moving from sphinx pose to down-dog now too. I only had eight turn up though I knew a few that couldn't make it. I'm still a bit worried the class might peter out over the summer months.

I came home and David had made a prawn and noodle stir-fry. I wasn't actually all that hungry but I ate it and a croissant all the same.

Thursday, 14th June

I am 27 weeks today and weighed myself nine stone 3 ¾ lbs – quite a surprise as I feel so much heavier than last week.

This morning was a bit challenging with the kids – Robbie crying and whining over the clothes I'd left out; Jane's friend gets dropped off at ours at the crack of dawn and has been upset going to school every day this week. When she arrived, Jane got upset as her friend said she was having a school dinner… and so it went on.

Well, the best part of today was when I was on my bike with my running client… I was all set to tell her that today would be her last session when she came with money for next week too. So next week will be the last week!

I had a rotten time with my daughter after school – a dispute over making a cake for her friends mum's birthday. Jane spent most of the afternoon and evening in her room for her cheek and bad behaviour. I don't know what's happened to the kids this week – maybe there is a full moon! I was exhausted by the time David came home and had decided to go straight to bed for a lie down once I had the kids in bed.

Friday, 15th June

I had my midwife appointment this morning – she took bloods to check iron levels and everything else was pretty much fine. My blood pressure was 110/70 which is normal for me. I did wake up with a strain in my chest, as if it was a cold but then as the day continued I started to think maybe I had strained a muscle or it was back pain.

I had three clients booked for today… One was in my house, as the weather had been wild and my client hadn't been keeping too well. I had salmon and salad before meeting my next client at Springburn Park and the weather was blowing a hoolie! I'd had a wee nap before this session and was feeling a bit better. We did 3 x 1miles broken up by core work – average pace just over 12 minute miling. I felt comfortable the whole time and it was good to be able to run and talk all the way. I know I said I'd stopped running altogether, but hey ho, I've came out of temporary retirement already! I just don't intend telling David or my mum as they won't be impressed.

My last client cancelled a few hours before the session due to work commitments, and though she would have been able to do half an hour later than arranged I had a race night with the school that I was going to. She offered to pay and on this occasion I suggested she just pay £15, though I felt bad about it as I couldn't offer her later or a session tomorrow as I stop at lunchtime. I've also said that next week will be my last session with this client as I'm stopping all evening work by the end of next week. I'm glad I've made this decision and I can relax more in the evenings.

The race night was good fun – mostly because jammy me won two races and the football card! In total I spent about £20 and won £56! There were hot snacks of pakora and sausage rolls and a few packets of Worcester sauce that I enjoyed too. It was a late night though – not in bed till near 12pm and I couldn't sleep easily because of a daft wee diet coke I'd had at the beginning of the night.

Saturday, 16th June

Well my normal Saturday morning fixture of circuits changed as I decided to cancel. The weather was wild, cold and wet and I was knackered after a late night and bad sleep – also still got a cold and really didn't want to be freezing for my ante-natal yoga class as the church hall is always cold enough. There were 4 girls that came so this was OK… One new girl that is expecting a week later than me.

I then had a client outdoors though the weather was dry and much calmer – she did a great session and I really love that I am motivating this client in all areas of her life.

The rest of the day was to be Father's Day as David is planning on working all day tomorrow. We all had lunch – I had the rest of the salmon with salad and baguette for lunch and a yogurt. We thought we'd all go out to David's parents for a bit and then out for a meal, but this just didn't happen as Jane had another tantrum about changing into a denim dress. It was another belter and it was good David was there to help deal with it as I've been so knackered today. As a consequence, we decided we weren't going anywhere. It was the right thing to do. I had a lovely relaxing bath as I just couldn't heat up after working outside. We just chilled out at home playing games, jigsaws and reading stories.

David is going to make a chicken curry (it is out of a jar but it will be lovely). Then it's an early romantic night for us… I think!

Sunday 17th June

Its Father's Day today though David has been at work most of the day. I got up and organised super early this morning. The kids were both showered, soup was made, washings were on and we managed to make it to mass too. Then we drove to David's work to pick him up and head to one of his Aunts for a look at some baby gear that was needing a home. We've now got a moses basket and plenty baby starter toys so it's been worthwhile to get my head in gear and think about what we need to still get.

We then headed over to David's mum and dads; his sister and full family also arrived with their two dogs. We haven't seen them since last year so it was nice to see them. My heartburn has been really rotten today and as soon as we got home I took one of the chalky tablets – they're disgusting. After some time at the park with the kids, it was home for dinner and more washings and ironings. I just had a cheese and banana toastie as the soup really did set off the heart burn. I'm sitting typing away and my legs are jumping all over the place just as this little baby is kicking furiously! I'm absolutely shattered, it's been a busy and productive day but I'm so glad the pressure is off for work now. I've really only got two weeks left now and then I'll only be working on the Saturday mornings.

Monday 18th June

We woke up to beautiful sunshine and it felt so good. Robbie had been up during the night, around 3am having a wee nightmare I think. He settled down really quickly though. I got up and instantly recognised heel pain in my right foot – likely onset of plantar fasciitis from wearing flat shoes more often and running on worn out trainers (and with being a heavier weight!) This is going to be my last week of work.

The kids had a good long lie in which was lovely! Sent off to school this morning and then Robbie and I went to the park to play and scoot! So that was at least one mile this morning of walking. I then went to the nursery's talk on car safety, for child safety week. It was all a bit worrying as I feel that we have put the kids in booster seats prematurely. So it's all change and I feel uncomfortable about the arrangements that the other mums, that share the school run, might have with seating too. At least, it's the end of the term and we can discuss arrangements for next year in a few weeks as I don't think I will be able to take five children, including our new baby, on the school runs.

After dropping Robbie off at nursery, I went for a walk at the park for about 40 minutes. I had a nap and then headed out to my two clients for the night. The first was in Glasgow and we did 20 minutes jogging and then a break for core work and then another 10 minutes jogging. Paces averaged at just over 11min/mile for the first part and just over 12min/mile for the second part. My second client was at the park and doing a little circuit, however she was so tired and was struggling with this; so we did a five min jog and two min walk twice followed by some core work. The midges were eating us like crazy, it was horrible. I feel much heavier tonight, I even felt the difference between the first and second client.

I came home and had beans on toast and a second FAB lolly, then a milky drink with some muesli oats! Feeling tired now and heading to bed.

Tuesday, 19th June

This morning, Robbie and I went to a CPR seminar at his nursery. It was so useful to have reminders for choking and CPR for babies and children. The best moment was when the trainer asked if anyone wanted a shot at getting the baby to choke out the object.Robbie's hand went up in the air as fast as ever! He gave the baby a cuddle and then tried slapping it on the back… then "Mummy" was to have a go. Well, I didn't do too well at that one but we both had a go at the CPR – it was great showing this to Robbie, though I'm hoping he doesn't start putting foreign objects into the baby's mouth and slapping it on the back!

I had my last time on my bike this afternoon with my client, so it really does feel like I'm slowing down now! After picking up the kids, I had a bit of a rough time of it with Jane again. She can be so cheeky and defy everything I say. I really gave her a good telling off but it left me pretty upset.

I had friends over for dinner tonight – I used to work with them back when I worked in the council. It was a good night, I made lasagne and one had brought apple pie and ice-cream. It was a late night too; I didn't get to bed till about 11.30pm and it took me a while to fall asleep.

Wednesday, 20th June

I took Robbie to his "Musical Step" class – it was the last one today for the summer break and he got a balloon and bubbles which delighted him. I got a piece of tablet which I wouldn't normally eat but did really enjoy it with a cuppa!

I had a nice walk in the woods and then had a 20 minute nap before picking up Jane. We went to the shops to get me new bras out of ASDA – only £3 for a bra isn't bad! They fit well too and even though I feel and look massive, I'm still fitting their 36B/C cup!

I spoke with my sister today and heard her good news that she is also pregnant – 12 weeks, though it looks like she might have an infection and this is worrying. Praying all will work out fine.

I went to my yoga class tonight as a student. The class was really good but there were only three people that turned up so I was really disappointed. I'll send a message around everyone though I think it will be abandoned till I return next year.

I came home and ate a full vegetable pizza and then had baked apple, dates and cream! I wasn't even hungry. Pure greed. Well, I really need to go to bed now as my twitchy itchy legs and heartburn are so uncomfortable.

Thursday, 21st June

I'm 28 weeks today and well the scales had gone up a fair bit (no wonder!) Now at nine stone 5 ¾ lbs. I've had a pretty good day. I did the ironing this morning then took Robbie to a soft play for a wee while before his nursery. Then I went for a swim – I did 60 lengths in about half an hour, usual pace, but it felt good. Then I picked everyone up from school with the intent of Jane going to her hair appointment, only to find that it was closed. Well I took it upon myself to cut her fringe… I've well and truly cut it! It's about an inch above her eyebrows… But she loves it!

She had a disco at the school tonight and she was so excited that I thought I'd better calm them down with a film. I put on Jungle Book 2 from when I'd recorded it at Christmas time. They loved it. Jane got very excited about her disco, dancing around like she was on Duracell batteries! She came home having won a prize for best dancer… So I was pleased for her. She also got her school report today for P1 and this was really good and positive too.

Friday, 22nd June

Well, this is pretty much my last day of working during the day and in the evenings, apart from my Saturday mornings. The day started off dry and very muggy. Robbie and I went out with him on his bike; followed by lunch of a salmon sandwich before his nursery.

The weather took a turn for the worse when I was at work with thunder and lightning. I ended up training my client under a big leafy tree, it was not really a safe option! She surprised me with a big, beautiful bouquet of flowers. I feel really lucky to be in a job that I love, but also where I make new friends. We cut the session early by about 10 minutes and the heavens opened.

I did some yoga practise at home in preparation for my client tonight. The weather had cleared up for my next client at 4.30pm however the rain then started again and didn't stop till we stopped the session. We ran for 30 minutes, averaging at 12 min/mile – I've surprised myself that I've still been able to run pretty comfortably at 28 weeks, however this will be my last run (yes, I know I've said that before!) We got soaked, and then I had my last client at her home doing yoga. I must've smelled really musty and damp, but she did a great wee session and again I felt really good and able to do most of what I was demonstrating. I ended up being out with this client for another half hour, having a blether and saying cheerio.

My shower never felt better and then David had made a steak dinner which went down pretty well. I then just sat on Facebook writing about the day and saying thanks to my clients.

Saturday, 23rd June

Well, my normal fixture of circuits changed this morning as there was only going to be one paying client turning up and a friend so I took the decision to cancel. The client decided she wanted a PT session so this was a win-win situation for me. The antenatal yoga class was brilliant – five turned up, including David's cousin, and she is lovely. It's great to be doing something I love, that benefits pregnant women and myself… And I get paid to do it!

I then did the weekly shop – £126! It's going to take a jump up when this baby arrives that's for sure! Jane was at a friend's party and David had some daddy time with Robbie (he bought him new Lightning McQueen trainers). David then had to go to work as he has taken on a worker during the week and training him is taking up his time.

I did a therapeutic clean-out of my car while the kids played with pals on the street – all the weights came out the boot as I'll only be working on the Saturdays now. It actually feels quite good! I've got this week Monday – Thursday off while the kids are at school and nursery and this is my time to get on with tax return paperwork and any extra time will be chill-out time.

I've had a great wee day, kids have behaved, housework has been done and I've made a pasta chicken dish for David coming home any time now… though he's late, it's 8.20pm. Football is on telly and I'm enjoying watching this to zone out. I also treated myself to a wee magazine today to reward myself for finishing work.

Sunday, 24th June

Thankfully, the kids slept till after 7am though David was up and away by 5.30am to London. I'm still feeling knackered though. The weather looked pretty optimistic this morning so I headed out with a packed lunch to Mugdock Country Park – we had a brilliant time. The kids loved the play park and the forest adventure challenges; the sun was out and it was warm. I couldn't have asked for a better day, children behaved so well and we just took the day moment by moment. We came home and I had a wee 20-minute nap while they watched some telly.

David came home and we all ate dinner together – burgers in a brown roll with salad… This was lovely though I wasn't hungry. Maybe something to do with the fact I ate a cinnamon twirl and a hot chocolate when we got home!

David's bathing the kids while I put my feet up and then I'm going to chill out and maybe watch the England game… And why not!

Well, went to bed and checked my mobile phone that had been charging to find two messages that led to me having a pretty rubbish sleep. My neighbour had locked their 16-week-old baby in the car by accident (the car locks automatically) and had to break the window to try and get into the car.

The next message was an email reply from a new enquiry about the antenatal yoga. It turns out this mum is expecting her second daughter two weeks after we are due, but has tragically just lost her 20-month-old daughter in March. This is just beyond grief and understanding – I just don't know how you can cope with this loss and be pregnant and expecting again. Some people are so strong. I've offered her some one-to-one sessions in her home to get her started as she can't make this week and I'll be on holiday the next two.

Monday, 25th June

This is the last week of school and nursery; the sun was shining and I took Robbie to the park. We had a great time for a few hours, he was so well behaved

– he didn't even complain when kids stood on his sandcastles and when he fell off his scooter trying to do fancy tricks. I just adore my kids.

The day was pretty boring after this – after the nursery run I put my car in for a service and got stung by the bill, nearly £400! I had to wait on the car so I had a look around the nearby retail park. I've been so tired today I just gave up after looking twice in Mothercare at the buggies. I headed to TESCO and bought a baby magazine and went to their café for a diet coke and a packet of crisps. My head has been sore again and I just have felt drained all day.

David came home about 7.30pm tonight and we ate an omelette for dinner – it was lovely. Our baby has been so active tonight – he/she feels really big and with little space to move, some of these kicks are really starting to feel uncomfortable.

I'm heading upstairs to bed now (9.45 pm) but it will probably be nearer 10.30pm before I'm in bed and settled!

Tuesday, 26th June

I don't know where this month has gone, but it's getting really scary how fast time is flying in. The sun was out and it was a beautiful morning so I took Robbie to a Country Park. He made a few new friends, kidding on they could see the Gruffalo in the forest. One friend was someone he knew from nursery and it turns out he'll be going to school in August and starting in Jane's composite class too.

After lunch (hummus and cheese sandwich) and the nursery run I went a walk at the local park. I can't believe how suddenly I feel knackered and I was walking much, much slower than usual. I think because time is going so fast I feel that I should be able to do everything I was doing last week or the week before. The mere thought of jogging seems unreal and it was less than a week ago I did 30 minutes' jogging.

I came home and managed a quick 20-minute nap – I really didn't want to get up and could quite happily have stayed in bed for a few good hours! After school, a few of the neighbours' kids were round and I heard that their mum has just discovered she is about 6 weeks pregnant. I met another mum in the street this morning with her five-month-old daughter – she was asking about personal training and fitness.

I made spaghetti and meatballs for dinner and demolished most of Robbie's too… Followed by my Gaviscon tablets! I am so tired tonight I just want to go to bed just now, and it's not even 8pm. I am determined to try some yoga though as my back has been aching these last few hours.

Well I did manage 45 minutes of yoga and it did the trick!

Wednesday, 27th June

Well, this is the last full day of school and nursery for the kids before the holidays. I've just felt like a shuttle service all day today – dropping Jane at school then Robbie at nursery then Jane from school. Then, I was no sooner home and I had a call the nursery about Robbie and his wheeze and rosy red face. So I picked him up and by the time we'd got there, his face had cooled down (they sat him next to the fan!) and he was running around full of beans. I took him to the doctor anyway and had his wheeze checked out – nothing serious just to keep giving him his inhaler. In the middle of all the driving around, I managed to fit in a good 45-minute walk at the park.

Things weren't doing too badly until Jane had a big hissy fit over tidying up mess she'd left before trying on her new dancing clothes. She ended up screaming at the top of her voice, 'I hate you,' outside the toilet door that I was in… Then kicking it. Needless to say, she was put in her bedroom. However, I managed to stay really calm. She didn't calm down very quickly and I had to go to work. When I came in about 9.30pm tonight, I found out she'd fallen asleep and not even had her dinner! This has never happened.

I had an antenatal yoga session with an amazing mum who's just lost her 20-month-old baby girl, and is expecting two weeks after we are. There are no words to describe how much grief she and her husband are going through, and her daughter was such a beautiful, beautiful girl.

I then went to the last "yoga for everyone" class – there were seven this week and a few new people, however, I've already decided to put it on hold now until I return, hopefully in January!

I came home and had a few bowls of cereal, sent several texts back and forward to my sister about bras and feeling big, before heading off to bed.

Thursday, 28th June

29 weeks today and scales say nine stone 6lb – the weight sure is piling on now! The day didn't start well at all and unfortunately this hung over me all day. David lost his temper with Jane to a point I thought was really excessive and well

out of proportion. Sadly, we were rowing in front of the kids and I was really annoyed that David had got everyone so upset at only 7.15am!

Doing the school run, I was just waiting on Jane getting upset again and again – especially as everyone was arriving with presents for the teacher leaving. I kept reminding Jane that she had made her a card and that this was special too. She seemed to accept this.

Robbie and I got right into clearing out some wardrobes and the spare bedroom. I can't believe how much I have cleared out (two bags for charity) and now we have drawer space for the baby's clothes! Anyone would think I was nesting as I've got right into cleaning and tidying today. I've also been as crabbit as a dog with the kids. I really think it's because of the way the day started.

I took a quick drive to the chemist to get my special sanctuary face cream – it's called "stop the clock" and I think it's amazing stuff. I also treated myself to a meal deal – had some Moroccan chicken cous cous salad which was lovely, and I've got a piece of carrot cake in the fridge that I still might have.

Jane's school finished at 1pm, so I picked her up then and not to my surprise, she was guzzling chocolate that the teacher had given out. We pretty much stayed in this afternoon until after the kids' dinner, when they went out to play in the street (I'm always there with them). A neighbour came home with her four-year-old boy and 18-month-old daughter so the kids wanted to play with them a bit longer. I let them stay out till about 6.30pm before asking them to come in for their bath. The neighbour lets her son stay up till after 10pm some nights and then sleep as long as he needs. I think she must think I'm super strict but I'd rather have the routine we have – it works well when they go to school too and the kids are shattered by bedtime anyway. She was talking about how her son was late in bed last night as he was on his iPad! I just don't get it! Why should a 4-year-old have an iPad? Give them a jigsaw! I find it really hard to hold my tongue and not give them my real thoughts but hey, we all have different ideas. They probably feel the same about me.

Friday, 29th June

David was up early to go to London today and the kids were up equally early at 6.15am. David got them breakfast. I'm still mad at him… He doesn't think he's done anything wrong and never apologises. I really don't like his statement that "It's my fault if Jane is like this all her life!" He really doesn't see the bigger picture; his shouting is creating problems too. Ah well. I'm used to it just being me and the kids most of the time anyhow and it's easier that way if all he does is shout when they are less than perfect.

After the normal routine of getting up and organised, I decided to clear out the kids' wardrobe. I probably shouldn't have as I've not been feeling too great again today – I've had that really metallic taste in my mouth and felt sick, headachy and a little dizzy. I checked my blood pressure and it was 106/64 so a bit lower than normal. I had a wee 20-minute nap with the kids watching telly, then we headed round to our neighbours' boy's fourth birthday party. The kids had a great time. Jane has been much better behaved and I've been doing a little colouring-in incentive chart today for any good behaviour.

After coming home from the party, I really didn't feel good again and needed another lie down on the couch – I must have dozed off, despite Olivia Newton John blaring and the kids making a mess all around me! This was a longer nap but I did feel a bit better for it and read to the kids for nearly an hour after it. They had pizza for tea and I had a few slices followed by a half salmon and mayonnaise sandwich.

David came in just at the right time (6.30pm) for me to get out to my first art class at the Dennis studio. This was good and has got me inspired to start sketching again over the next week. I got a great deal through "living social" network – 12 x 2 hour sessions for £48 – you can't knock that. I've had pretty bad heartburn tonight and my baby has been sitting really uncomfortably with strong kicks. My back is also pretty sore – I didn't have any of these problems in my other pregnancies. I think these last 10 weeks or so might be very uncomfortable.

Saturday, 30th June

I had cancelled circuits class yesterday thinking I wasn't feeling quite up to it, and then this morning the weather was fine and dry and it turns out there would have been at least four turn up. Aw well, I've made that decision that I've finished the circuits now till I return next year! I went a walk instead for about 45 minutes and then went to my antenatal yoga class which I really enjoyed. Only four could make it but it was a good class.

I wasn't long home before David and the kids came home with the shopping. We all had lunch and then after some chill out time we headed to a Country Park. There's been a lot of heavy rain off and on all day and it was great being in the forest with the kids and staying dry at the same time. In David's own words, he admits it did him the world of good and was what he needed to help him switch off and also get some exercise.

We then headed to a Brewers Fayre for dinner. I had fish and chips and a half pint of lager shandy. It was great – a real wee treat. Now I'm just chilling out watching Andy Murray playing on Wimbledon.

Sunday, 1st July

Today started off with some housework – usual washings and ironings. Then I took the kids to the park – they played for a while in the play park and then we had a picnic lunch before having a go on the scooters. I had to climb up to the top of a climbing frame to rescue Robbie – it was the first time he had climbed to the top and he was a bit upset about getting back down. I didn't feel that great about climbing up and holding Robbie with one hand and trying to balance myself all the way down!

The next drama was with the scooters. Jane and Robbie scooted off too fast and I couldn't even see them round the corners. I had to run as fast as I could and I was so worried they had scooted right onto the road. When I finally caught up with them, they got a right telling off and we went straight home. I felt really sore in my pelvis and feel I've got the onset of pubis synthesis dysfunction. I was shattered and the rest of the day I've felt pretty sore. The other main pregnancy symptom that's been getting worse is the heartburn. I'm taking a Gaviscon tablet after everything I eat.

David finished work for 2pm which was nice and we had a family trek to The Pram Centre to look at prams. There is such a selection and I just felt so knackered that I had no interest in making decisions. I felt a bit dizzy and ropey again and had to have a wee seat. David bought me some coke to drink which seemed to do the trick. By the time we got home and I checked my blood pressure it seemed to be fine.

We had a chicken stir-fry dinner, followed by strawberries and cream and then later before bed I had toasted banana and cream (I was hungry again!). We watched the Spain v Italy final of the European cup and it was fantastic – I'm really enjoying chilling out and watching all the sport on telly!

Monday, 2nd July

I had great plans to take Jane to a dance class every day this week from 11-12pm… Thinking it was local. Well, it turned out it was in Thornliebank and a bit of a long journey though Jane really enjoyed it. She was all dressed in her little leotard, skirt and ballet shoes and all the rest of the kids were in their tracksuits and trainers!

Then we headed to meet my yoga pal at People's Palace. She has two girls about Jane's age. It turns out the People's Palace is closed on Mondays though at least the café was open. The kids all had a great time running around the gardens and having an ice-cream (though Robbie was the child that dropped his... He didn't seem that bothered)

Then we headed to the kids' play park. We weren't long there when the heavens opened and we took shelter under the pirate ship. The kids were still playing in the sand making sand cakes and getting wetter and wetter. Eventually, we just bit the bullet and headed home, cleaning our hands and shoes in the puddles. It took me ages to get home from there – I just kept getting lost and going round and round in circles. At least we got out, despite the weather. Once we were home, we changed and the kids cosied up in front of the telly.

I did more computer work before I made the kids pasta bolognaise for dinner, David and I will have it later.

Tuesday, 3rd July

Today has been a pretty good day with the kids. I took Jane to a multisport session, lasting two hours. I'm so proud that she just settles into the class despite not knowing anybody – and she loved it. Robbie and I just went to ASDA to get groceries and things we needed before heading back to pick up Jane.

The rest of the day we just played about the house. The kids played out on the street, though I wasn't overly impressed that the older kids (mostly aged eight-nine years) were wanting to play with them. I'd rather they played with kids their own age. I said this a few times to the kids, with limited success. I've been half expecting their mum to come and knock on the door about it!

We all had different dinners tonight – I had salmon, potatoes, broccoli and peas; Jane had scrambled egg and potatoes; and Robbie had cheesy beans and potatoes! I then had strawberries and yogurt though I'm thinking about having something else. At lunchtime, I had a big salad and a wholemeal bagel, followed by a cup of tea and a milky way. I've had melon, apple and strawberries today.

Since the kids went to bed, I've been sitting trying to work out this new account and ISA stuff and it's just driving me crazy – I can't believe how many forms and how much mail I've received daily about transferring money, opening an account and everything else. My head hurts and the baby is kicking so strongly that I feel like bed. My hopes of doing my online self-assessment tonight will have to wait. On a positive, I have entered a few competitions to win prams and car seats, fingers crossed!

Wednesday, 4th July

I like the pace of the school holidays – in the morning there is no sense of urgency to get organised and ready for school. The kids are still getting up too early to justify them staying up later. David had come in about 10.30pm last night and I had watched Little Man Tate till after 11pm. David got up with the kids at about 6.30am and gave them breakfast, which was a nice gesture.

We didn't do a hell of a lot this morning apart from playing in the house and usual housework. I did review a food diary for an expectant mum who comes to the antenatal class and she was happy with the help. Then I took the kids to the train station for a go on their scooters. We met an old man, Jack, out walking with his dog. I see a lot of Jack. I remember the first time I met him about four years ago, when I was out with Robbie as a baby in his pram. Jack had put a few pounds in his pram. Jack and his wife Jean are in their 80s and sadly both suffer from cancer. He is using crutches to walk his dog four times a day, though today he told me the pain is constant and unbearable. But he still has a sense of humour and laughed when he told me about breaking his finger recently when he fell in the cemetery. He'd said he couldn't get up but at least he was better off than everyone else in the graveyard!

We came home and had lunch (salmon salad for me) and then headed to the shops to buy some waterproof trousers for the kids, pregnacare vitamin tablets and my "Mum-to-be" bounty bag from BOOTS. Then I met with my sister-in-law and we all went to the soft play for a few hours. It was really clammy today and lots of heavy showers in between the heat… I quite like this weather!

The kids were great today though. I've felt pretty good although it's now nearly 9pm and I'm contemplating bed. David came home by 6pm tonight to see the kids and then we had a prawn noodle stir-fry. It was a TV dinner as we watched as Andy Murray made it through to the semi-finals of Wimbledon. I finished off a milky way and a hot chocolate. As usual I've had loads of fruit today so the healthy everything else offsets the little bit of chocolate! I should be trying to do some yoga, but struggling to fit it in and I've been feeling tired just dancing around the room with Jane in the morning! I do feel a lot of pressure down on my pelvis with this baby. My sister-in-law commented that she thought I was bigger than I was with Robbie.

Well, I've managed to do a good 45 minutes of yoga practise and feeling really good about that… Maybe not so happy with my bedtime of nearer 11pm again.

Thursday, 5th July

I'm 30 weeks today! I can't believe it. My weight this morning was nine stone 5½lbs, so not a weight gain this week – I guess it really depends how much I've been eating in the last few days too!

I've had a really tiring day today. David was up and away early and the kids woke at 6am! It seems to be getting earlier and I just send them back to their room and ask them to go to bed… They did for about half an hour and then they just get up and play. Usually, they get on well playing together but something happened this morning that led to Robbie running into my room upset and saying Jane had bitten him! She has never bitten before and I really wasn't sure what was going on. Jane said she had nipped him and he agreed; she was given a very serious telling off and apologised to Robbie. I let it go, but later in the afternoon I noticed a bruised blood mark on his back roughly where he'd said she'd bit him. So the drama was revisited.

So that was first thing this morning. They both played fine after this and then we took Jane to her multisport session. Robbie and I just went to the shops and bought a few extras for the holiday and some baby doll underwear for me (nothing too sexy though, but nice all the same). We then caught five minutes of Jane at the end of her session doing a little dance routine on her own… I was so proud, she still looks so small compared to all the others. She said she loved it and that they did yoga and then the hip hop dancing!

This afternoon my cousin visited with her two little ones. Sadly, they had had another little boy and he didn't make it after a long and difficult birth. I realised my due date was maybe about the same time as his anniversary and it turns out he was born on the 12th and died on the 14th. I really hope our baby is born before these dates.

Jane was proving to be really cheeky this afternoon and just trying to defy everything I was saying. I don't know whether she was just trying to show off but I was close to expecting a full-blown tantrum from her. When our visitors had left, I said there would be no telly and no garlic bread with the dinner. I had bought a healthy ready meal of sweet potato and spinach lasagne… Neither of the kids were that impressed with it. They got brown bread and butter and salad and were encouraged to eat at least a few more mouthfuls!

I must be nesting – I deep cleaned the fridge tonight but couldn't get the shelves back in – don't think the fridge has been cleaned since before Robbie was born. Ah well, it probably won't happen ever again now as this is definitely the last baby I'll be having.

After a bath and bed, I was relieved to have some quiet time to myself. It's now after 10pm – David has sent a text saying he'll be much later tonight and I'm still sitting up working away. I've written up a programme for a client tonight and been responding to enquiries about the antenatal yoga and just keeping in touch with a few people.

I sent a little message to the client that lost her little girl and she so sadly replied about what had happened in an email. It's just beyond grief what they must be going through.

Friday, 6th July

I didn't have the best night's sleep – I went to bed too late (after 11pm) and then David didn't come home till 2am. I couldn't quite switch off from the thoughts of the last email and then I was woken at 5am by some noise up on the roof. The day didn't start off too well with the kids… Constant bickering, fighting and crying and up at 6am again. I maybe didn't deal with it all too well either. I think they are just so excited about going on holiday.

We picked up my mum from the bus station – I drove into Buchanan bus station and was ferried out by the conductors; I didn't realise that no cars are allowed in.

The kids' behaviour improved greatly and they were well excited to see their gran and thinking about the holiday ahead. We all had lunch and then I got onto doing some packing while my mum entertained the kids. I watched Federer beat Djokovic in the semi-final of Wimbledon and then had a nap as I was feeling pretty tired and my back was aching. When I got up, I started to feel achy and my buttocks and legs were also really tired. Jeez, I really sound like I'm struggling in this pregnancy.

We all had pizza for dinner and then I went to my art class. This is my second week and we did another upside-down drawing on perspective, this time of a stool. It's good to get a bit of time to myself but I just missed seeing Andy Murray win his semi-final against Tsonga. It makes you feel really good – apparently a Brit hasn't made it to the finals in 74 years! That's some achievement.

Since I came home, my mum and David have had a nice wee night drinking red wine. I'm hoping again for an early night and this is just not looking like it's happening… It's now nearly 11pm, though that's me finished for now. Holidays tomorrow!

Saturday, 7th July

Jane was up at 5am last night, and after firmly saying "Bed", she burst into tears and then had a horrible coughing fit… She sounded terrible and at that moment I had a thought that I would need to be taking her to the "out of hours" in the morning. They both must have gone back to sleep, though I struggled to sleep again. It was just after 6am when I felt like I was getting back to sleep when I heard them both up. They quietly went in to see their gran and as she was OK with this; I stayed in bed till just about 7am. We all had breakfast, David managed a lie-in until about 8.30.

We set off about 9.30am and arrived at the cottage in St Andrews just before 11.30am – lucky for us it was all ready as we were advised the entry time would be 2pm. The owner had left some lovely fresh cream fairy cakes… Robbie's skin got a little bit sore after this but soon cooled down again after some medicine. After a short time on the beach looking for crabs, the rain came on and we headed back.

We had baked potatoes and I had tuna salad while the kids had cheese and beans. We headed back out along the craggy rocks and coastal path for some more fresh air, in the hope that the kids would get tired! A bath later and they were in bed for 8pm, but Robbie was still talking to his new "friend", Spiderman, nearly an hour later. Me and my mum just sat chilling out in the evening – she was reading her book while I did my usual PC stuff. I'm so used to my own company in the evenings, I'm not even feeling much up to chatting all night with my mum. Looking forward to going to bed in fact! I've been so itchy with a lot of my clothes again tonight, I'd rather be tucked up in bed than try and fight it. I heard good news that my friend in the street had her twins – a boy and a girl.

Well, by the time I got to bed, it was after 11pm again, talking to my Mum. Really need to get an early night tomorrow.

Sunday, 8th July

Jane was coughing badly at about 6am again this morning and everyone really was awake by then. She came in with me for a little while and then my mum and I got back to sleep till just after 7am which was nice.

We had a nice slow start and then headed out – it actually got quite warm and the kids had a great time playing in the sand and having a picnic. After that, we went to Craigtoun park and had a shot on the mini railway and adventure park before heading home. Mum and I had hoped to see some of the Wimbledon tennis final with Andy Murray however the kids started to play up a bit and the telly was put off for a while.

We then headed out for dinner – I had a big chicken burger with cheese and bacon and chips (it's hardly worth mentioning the salad!). I couldn't believe how much there was, and this was followed by a high tea! I just had a cup of tea and a wee slice of franzipan cake. Robbie loved the pancakes and even though he'd eaten a lot of his dinner he still managed to lick a second pancake to claim it and eat it!

Since coming home, I've felt so tired. I am so much bigger in this pregnancy than previous ones and my back has been hurting on and off today. I feel it would be nice to go for a long walk and it's strange for me not to have been doing exercise.

I'm going to head for bed by 9pm tonight as I know Jane is probably going to be in my bed later.

Monday, 9th July

I had probably my best sleep in about 6 months last night, but am feeling a bit guilty since it turns out my mum had Jane in with her for most of the night. I hadn't heard a thing, though in fairness, I had closed over the doors a bit more than before. Jane had been coughing again so my mum thought it best to have her in with her, before she woke up Robbie and me. Don't think my Mum got much sleep last night.

The weather dried up this morning and we got to the beach. Jane has been pretty cheeky and difficult most of the day, just trying to stir things up with her brother and do the opposite to what she was asked. Apart from that, we did have a good day. I phoned David and the kids got a chance to speak with him which I think gave him a nice surprise. I'm looking forward to him coming over tomorrow night, it'll be good to have half the holiday with him, though totally different and in some ways maybe more stressful when the kids don't behave.

I got the chance to have a wee walk on my own, along the coastal route this afternoon (while the kids saw a bit of telly). I did feel like my pelvic pain was there a little and so it wasn't a brisk walk by any means. It's strange to think I'm doing so little exercise now. We all just had lunch back at the cottage – I had oatcakes, cous cous and hummus salad and then me and my mum had salmon and salad for dinner (the kids had fishfingers and beans).

The kids were hilarious at bedtime tonight. They were chatting for over an hour in their beds about how they had a baby in their tummy and it was kicking lots... 'Do you want to see?' Then they were going to the "hospital" the day after tomorrow to have their baby. Then it was the names – Robbie called his Mamie though I shouted upstairs is this a girl or a boy and he said it was a boy! His baby turned out to be a soft toy red crab that was a gift from his gran today and he'd earlier named "Crabby"! What a laugh – it's the best they've got on all day!

I was drinking coke tonight as I wanted something sweet and then I had a piece of millionaire's shortbread. I'm heading to bed now, I just want to get as much sleep in as I can.

Tuesday, 10th July

The day didn't start too well... My mum has been sleeping on a sofa bed in the lounge area and so she's the first place the kids are going to when they get up in the morning. I got up just about 7am but was up about 3.30am and couldn't sleep for a while – I was thinking over some baby names in my head.... Thought of Beth and Drew, but I can just imagine David's thoughts!

Not long after breakfast, my mum saw how challenging Jane really can be – I suggested she put on her fleece as she's still got this cough and was feeling pretty cold. She grunted and quickly became a little horror, saying 'I hate you!' to me. My mum hasn't seen this behaviour and I was pretty shocked as it was so early in the day and came totally out of the blue. She was marched upstairs and she continued to shout this at me. I couldn't hide how I felt in front of my mum, and she didn't say much... Just something about it bringing back memories. Thanks Mum, not what I needed to hear.

I decided I would take Robbie swimming and my mum could do what she liked with Jane in the morning. My mum is always being very careful about not getting involved in any arguments; unfortunately, by saying nothing and not backing me up it's like she condones the bad behaviour. It's a difficult one but I'd rather be supported, and although I sometimes think David is too hard and shouts a bit too quickly, it's just as bad having another adult not supporting me. Jane clearly has cottoned on to this one and thinks she can get away with anything with her gran around.

I had a great wee time at the swimming with Robbie and on the way home he was sleeping within five minutes. We picked up Mum and Jane and went to the cheese factory for lunch. I had a lovely salmon and white cream cheese spread on soda bread and with salad, it was delicious.

I suggested my mum get some time to herself to look at the shops. Jane was very well behaved when it was just me and Robbie and then when we picked up my mum she started trying to push her luck. I made a little comment about Jane knowing exactly what she was doing and thinking she could get away with anything with her gran.

Things didn't get a whole lot better after dinner time when Jane was asked to get ready for bed and she just decided to cuddle into her gran and ignore anything I said. Once again, my mum said nothing and that was the final straw. I asked my mum to support me and she said, 'I'm not getting involved!' Well thanks, you are involved as Jane is thinking she can do what she likes! I said if she could at least reinforce what I'm saying, to which she said she knows what reinforcement is! It's been pretty hard work today and I felt really awkward in the evening. Not really up to much conversation.

I decided to get out a walk and have some time to myself while I could – it was a bit wet but I really enjoyed walking along the coastal path. I'd had bad news this morning about my friend; she's in hospital with viral meningitis after she was found barely conscious. This was on my mind all day too and the walk did me good to try and clear my thoughts. I was out for just over an hour and when I got in the kids had just been put to bed and were sleeping within the half hour.

David arrived not long after 8pm with a takeaway fish and chips and I quietly whispered in his ear not to bring anything up about the kids' behaviour and that I'd speak with him about it tomorrow. The fish and chips was pretty average for a fish shop that's meant to be the best in Scotland. There was so much batter and tiny wee chips – my first fish and chips in ages and I don't think I'm missing out on much.

Went to bed about 10.30pm – it's been so good to see David again, I realise how much I've missed him when I saw him.

Wednesday, 11th July

The kids slept better last night and were sleeping quicker than any other nights just by putting them to bed at their normal 7pm time. I didn't hear them until after 7am this morning but my mum told me Jane was up coughing during the night again. Well this was the last day for my mum and we drove her to the bus station and then went on to the swimming pool.

After lunch, we headed to meet friends at their holiday home and let the kids all play together. What a house, well mansion really, with a garden equally as big that led right onto the beach. We got the kids changed – though it was dry and sunny it was a bit chilly -this didn't stop them running and chasing each other into the sea. Their kids had wet suits but our two had leggings and shorts/t-shirt on! I really hope this doesn't make Jane much worse. If it wasn't for the fact they all had colds, they'd have been better off in the scud! The dads headed off to the pub for a pint while we walked back along the beach to get the kids ready to go out for an ice-cream. They had a great time and it was hilarious seeing them all in the shower being hosed down! They all had another play at the park and then an ice-cream with a flake – a first for Jane and Robbie.

We came back to our cottage and the plan was for homemade lasagne but I hadn't realised the beef was out of date and stinky. David now wants more chips for dinner but he's on his own! I'm having omelette and he's having his with chips while I have salad!

Thursday, 12th July

The kids slept better, hooray! Up after 6.30am, and not disturbed with any coughing during the night like I was expecting. Today, I've felt really tired, exhausted almost, despite getting plenty sleep. That's me 31 weeks today and getting a bit nervous now at how quickly time is passing, and how mentally unprepared I feel.

We all went out a walk and ended up on the beach… A few sandcastles later and a park and the kids were happy! I had a nap for a bit longer than my usual nap whilst David took the kids out to get milk. When I woke up, the sun was out and it was very warm… It didn't stay out long and we ended up walking around the shops and buying the kids another wee treat. Robbie started insisting he wanted to go back to his old home and acting really whiny. We're hoping he's not heading for what Jane's had, though at least Jane's behaviour has been a lot better and she seems to be getting over the cough.

We ended up having dinner out – I had a massive aubergine, goats cheese and salad dinner – it was delicious, but too too much! David had been to a chocolatier earlier today and bought me some dark chocolate – I was a bit annoyed with him for buying it as it wasn't even made there, it was just like a bar out the supermarket but it cost £4.50! Think I'm just feeling a bit anxious now.

David's planning on going out on his bike now, it's nearly 8pm and he's hardly got any bright clothes or a helmet to wear. I'm just going to chill out with the telly… Changed days but I'm too stuffed to do any yoga!

Friday, 13th July

It was my chance to get a wee extra hour in bed so I didn't get up till just after 8am. Today, we spent the day in Crail – a lovely little seaside town where we spent more time on the beach, fishing for crabs, playing in the park and trying to fly a kite! One thing's for sure – the kids have had loads of fresh sea air and a run around! I made the most of David being here and took any opportunity I could to sit my bum on a bench.

We had a nice lunch, I had potato and leek soup and later a packet of crisps. Dinner was homemade lasagne and I feel thoroughly stuffed. I'm going to head on out for a walk now.

Well that was great, I felt I had more energy than earlier and walked briskly for about 40 minutes.

Saturday, 14th July

Homeward bound – everything packed and cleaned and then we hit the road. David took the kids and I headed off on my own for some peace. I got back not long after 11am and started cleaning out my car! Of all things… Never mind the unpacking, I just had to hoover out the car and get rid of some of the sand!

After lunch, more unpacking and then cleaning toilets and everything else. It's been a good day, I can't believe how excited the kids were to be coming home this morning. I can't imagine being away for more than a week – it is always nice to get home.

David made a roast chicken and vegetables for dinner – he wasn't too happy that I said it was alright… Well it was, I'm not going to lie! It wasn't that tasty. I was shattered after dinner and even tried a bit of yoga, but had to stop… Way too tired. Headed up to bed at 9pm to watch Casualty – wish I hadn't bothered it was rubbish. I must've fallen asleep really quickly as David said he came to bed at 10.30pm and I didn't hear him at all.

Sunday, 15th July

I've had a really good day though looking back on it I don't feel I did much. The days all feel the same so it doesn't really feel like a Sunday today. David was at work all day though he plans to come home around 9pm. We went to supermarket for some things David had missed this morning and then popped into BOOTS to get a gift voucher for our neighbour with new-born twins.

My sister-in-law came round after lunchtime and we stayed in and had a good catch-up. She's not long back from travelling and fundraising.

At dinner I was extra greedy. I felt really, really tired and so had a pizza that I'm sure David had bought for himself to eat. A big cheesy meatball thing and I ate the lot!

I went straight to bed for a lie down after the kids were down and didn't get back up till 8.45pm. I still feel shattered and sluggish, probably all the carbs. I've since had a small glass of shandy, oh dear. I know if I went to bed just now I'd sleep no problem. I'm even contemplating having some left over chocolate chip muffins from this afternoon. It's a good job I don't eat like this very often eating.

Monday, 16th July

I got a good 8 hours' sleep (with only one toilet break in the middle of the night) and I'm still not ready for getting up at about 6.30am when the kids are up. David left before 5.30am and I have no memory of him getting up or leaving… Normally I hear his alarm.

I took Jane to another out of school sports session in Chryston this morning, thinking there might be some friends from school. It was really noisy before she even went in and she seemed to be the youngest there. Although she said she enjoyed it she said she preferred the other one so she can go back to the Tuesday and Thursday arrangement and forget about this one. Robbie and I went to the park on his scooter – I really notice a change in what I can do this week. Even walking is posing some discomfort for me and I'm beginning to worry that I've done too much exercise throughout this pregnancy, or maybe it's just that this baby is bigger and it's more uncomfortable. I'll hopefully manage to get some swimming in and enjoy feeling weightless.

Once we'd picked up Jane and had lunch, I needed a sleep so unfortunately the kids were parked in front of the telly. I had about 25 minutes or so and it made all the difference. We all played in the house for a while but then I realised I really needed more Gaviscon for the heartburn, but the local chemist is closed for the Glasgow fair holiday. On the way to the shops, we saw the neighbours out for a walk. They offered to take the kids while I went to the shops – even that wee half hour to myself was nice.

For dinner, I had a big mackerel salad and washed down with the Gaviscon!

The kids have been pretty good today – Jane had a bit of a tantrum at bedtime though I was maybe a bit strict with her. She just kept fidgeting and getting up and down when I was trying to read the bedtime stories… Yes, in hindsight, I think I over-reacted, considering she was tired and she has been so good all day.

Well, I managed to do about 30 mins of yoga tonight – I am so tired I just want my bed and it's only 9pm.

Tuesday, 17th July

This morning, we took Jane and her friend to her multi-sports session while me and Robbie went to the Pram Centre. I couldn't get to sleep after waking at 3am and my head was going over and over thinking about how we didn't have a pram or a car seat! So, I was on a mission, but I still couldn't make up my mind. I decided to leave it and look online.

I later chose a Quinny pram from Mothercare and my pal is going to lend us a carrycot that will fit it too. OK so I'm getting somewhere! Kids were out playing in the garden later before the rain came back on heavy, so I had a wee chance to lie down – I was getting really crabbit with them again as I was so tired.

Dinner tonight was either chicken stir-fry for Robbie or prawn stir-fry for Jane and me. Robbie ate very little and so he was told to leave the table. Jane ate hers and had a wee chocolate biscuit before her bath. As did I… In fact I had a few chocolate crunchie biscuits.

Once the kids were in bed, I set about doing my self-assessment tax return. I've been putting it off forever and got a bit of a shock. I am so tired in the evenings I could well have just gone to bed at 8pm again. It turns out I hadn't updated my records since last July!! Blimey – it took me till 11pm just to write up my work and that was without labelling receipts or even starting to complete the self-assessment form online. That will need to be tomorrow night… Now that I've started I really have to get it done, that way we can see just what I owe and what money I need to make sure stays in that account. I went to bed about 11pm and David still wasn't home.

Wednesday, 18th July

What a lousy night's sleep I had… I felt like I saw every hour and my back was killing me. This pregnancy is now proving to be quite uncomfortable. Between the backache and heartburn, now my right heel is agony to walk on… I'm really looking forward to getting my body back already!

Normally, I want to get the kids outdoors walking at the park or on their scooters, but I've so little energy it's just as well it's rainy! Well, things had to be done so I took the kids to a shopping centre and got a bit of Jane's school clothes bought and then we went to M&S for some food for lunch and dinner. I couldn't get one sandwich that would have been suitable for Robbie – they either had mayonnaise in them or they were seeded rolls, so he had to wait till we got home. He was so good about it too. I had some random sushi thing with really peculiar flavours, not sure I enjoyed it. Also had a delicious fresh orange and lime drink too and bought a large piece of carrot cake to enjoy later.

My midwife appointment wasn't long after lunch though and sure enough, as I thought, the glucose levels were high in my urine – no surprise after that drink! The midwife took a blood check just to be sure and will let me know if it's too high tomorrow. It was lovely for Jane and Robbie to be involved again in hearing the baby's heartbeat. I've also been advised to phone the physio at the Infirmary about my foot and backpain. I think my heel pain might be referred pain from my hip and back – I got an appointment for next Friday.

The kids have been pretty well behaved today and have been sitting painting for the last 45 minutes while I type away!

They then ended up over at a neighbours' for a wee half hour and I got the chance to do some tidying and hoovering… Oh, joy, I should just have put my feet up! They had a pizza dinner and I had dinner later with David – it was a pasta dish from M&S as a wee treat and for convenience. This was the first night since Saturday that David has been home for dinner just after 7pm.

Thursday, 19th July

I had a better night's sleep though I am having loads of dreams… Really random non-important things that I can barely remember five minutes after I wake up (unless it's baby related!). My heel pain is agony in the mornings and my whole leg feels pretty weak and tingly. I made a doctor's appointment for later just in case I'm ignoring something I shouldn't be. It's frustrating to think that in my last pregnancies I was doing a lot of walking right up to the last few weeks and here I am wondering if I'm going to struggle to walk much more!

Took Jane to her last multi-sports session – she loved it and said she had been doing "Tae pon do" and dancing. I'm really happy she has been going to this no problem and not had any issues with being the youngest there, settling in and meeting other friends. After lunch, I took them both swimming and again Jane was doing well with swimming the back-stroke.

At the doctors I was given a topical mild analgesic for my heel and advised to take paracetamol. I was told it was unlikely just sciatic pain as it started from my heel. Really not looking forward to struggling to run or keep fit once our baby arrives. Speaking of which, our new Quinny pram arrived today! I want to make it up but think that might be bad luck.

The kids had a chance to play out the back this evening and it got quite warm so it feels like it's been a quick day. I finished my tax self-assessment today so just have a few questions I need to clear up over the phone.

My dinner tonight (David obviously at work) was omelette and salad, delicious. I did have a sneaky wee bar of chocolate that I'd bought out of M&S yesterday. I do seem to be having something sweet every day.

Well my mission is to get back into doing my yoga every day to see if it helps with all these aches and pains, so I managed to do a good 45-minute session tonight. Off to bed now, not long after 9pm!

Friday, 20th July

Well, I remembered to weigh myself this morning – seems the magazines are right about the weight gain! That's me at nine stone 8½ lbs… Think I got to nine stone 10lbs with Robbie so I'll be well overtaking that this time!

It's been a good day today. I booked my car in for an MOT and when I got there I realised it wasn't due till December! My neighbour had offered to take the kids so I made the most of it and asked the mechanic to check out the noise coming from the car – turns out one of the new shock absorbers from a few weeks ago has burst and is leaking. So I've got it booked in for a week on Saturday. I then got the food shop in for the week, in peace and quiet!

I spent a little bit of time round at my neighbours. The only other thing we really did was take the kids to the park as the weather was good – well, good enough that they wanted to take their socks and shoes off!

David came home at 5.30pm and I made a chicken and vegetable stir-fry with rice for us all. As usual, Robbie didn't eat his, saying he was too tired. So as usual, he got nothing else. David had the kids hyper by the time I left to go to my art class. I was ready for not going tonight as my back has been killing me, but I thought that if I didn't go then I probably wouldn't go back. I'm glad I went... There were a few new girls I hadn't met who were further on with their watercolour pictures and the chat was good. I've now drawn an outline of a Monet painting and am excited about going back and making a start on it on Monday night. Off to bed now though after a nice wee bowl of muesli... Hope I get a good night's sleep.

Saturday, 21st July

Well, as I'm writing this Sunday night, my memory of yesterday may be a little short! I know I did have a very good day. I had my antenatal yoga class and there were two new girls which was great. The yoga over the last few days has really helped me with my foot pain... Although I'm thinking the baby may just have shifted position since my heartburn has also eased off considerably.

After this, I came home to find David had done some hoovering and housework and had prepared a great packed lunch. We went to Almond Valley park – it's a farm and activity centre for the kids. We all had such a great time and it really tired out the kids.

David's mum came over to babysit later and we went to Frankie and Benny's for dinner – it was rubbish – I had a prawn salad and it was dreadful. I will never go back there as I always think that whatever I chose it is terrible and it's not even cheap! We then went to see The Angel's Share at the cinema – what a great, funny Glasgow film. I had plenty popcorn and chocolate revels to make up for the bad dinner. We sat up chatting to David's mum till about 11pm and then went to bed. She's about the only person who's really asked about baby names and she's usually the last person we should tell as she doesn't hold back on giving you her thoughts on what she likes!

Sunday, 22nd July

David has been at work all day. I did the done thing and took the kids to mass – I made sure I had paper and pens to keep them occupied! The rest of the day I had my mind set on doing lots of housework. I did manage some like the ironing and washings and clearing up, but I've still not done the toilets and the floors.

We did get out to the park for a little while in the afternoon, and this time the kids were well warned to not go off racing on their scooters. They were really well behaved, though my walking pace was a bit too fast for how I felt. I have been knackered all day. At least the kids have been good at playing together and tidying up.

I made a brilliant roasted salmon with veggies and salad for my dinner – don't be fooled though, I've already had iced ginger cake and dark chocolate and a biscuit today! But hey, it's about getting a balance. I had lots of blueberries and strawberries this morning and my muesli with seeds and all bran to start the day. At lunchtime we all had cheese and banana toasties – so I'd say that's a good mix of all the food groups!

Had my first bath in such a long time tonight and it was a delight. It's funny how with Jane and Robbies pregnancies they moved around a lot in the bath but this baby doesn't move quite as much.

David came home about 9.30pm and our conversation didn't last that long as I told him how I'd taken the kids to mass and let them do some colouring in. David doesn't think they should have anything with them to keep them occupied. Given the condition I am in and the need to limit Robbie jumping on me I think it's only fair I do what I can to make the experience easier for me. I was disappointed he didn't appreciate what I'd done a bit more.

Monday, 23rd July

The kids have been booked on a mini-kickers two hour football coaching session every day this week. I felt so proud of them both and how well they behaved, how little they looked, but how happy and involved they both were.

I have been so tired today as Robbie had been up several times during the night saying he was having a bad dream about the Gruffalo. I find it harder now to get back to sleep and our baby even woke me up at one point with the strength of the movement. I can't quite believe how strong these kicks or movements are, they are definitely stronger than the other two were and quite painful at times.

It was good to be able to just watch the kids at the football and relax for a wee while. We then went to my friends for lunch. She gave me back the cosy all-in-one suit we had taken Jane home from hospital in – this just took me back to that very precious moment and it was lovely telling this to Jane.

The kids have been so well behaved all day. After dinner, David arrived home and I headed out to my art class again (before David heads away on a stag weekend). I really enjoyed it and even though I'd felt like going to bed at 6pm, I felt better once I'd got there and started on my watercolour painting. I've actually brought it home to finish as it'll be almost two weeks till I can make it back again.

The baby has been moving a great deal since I've been home, my heartburn, although much better during the day, has returned a little just now and my legs are hell of a restless. That said, my heel and foot has almost made a miraculous recovery, so I can only imagine it must be to do with the positioning of baby. Well it's sleep for me now… Just after 10.30pm.

Tuesday, 24th July

I can't believe the kids slept till 7.45am this morning! Keep that up please and that will be great. I took them to their football practise and it was so cute to watch them paired up and in their oversized team vests. A friend came round for lunch with her two girls and they all had a great time playing. All great behaviour again which has been so much easier.

Once the kids were in bed, I went to bed too for a power nap. Then I did half an hour of yoga as I really know this is helping with all my aches and pains and symptoms. I read today that when the baby settles into birthing position often some of the symptoms get better, like heartburn. I think this has been the case!

I didn't really get an appetite for dinner tonight so just had toast and then later had some strawberries and ice-cream. My legs have been so jumpy again tonight, it's been hard to resist not going to bed altogether. As usual, though I've been on the PC looking at Facebook and emails… I've had another enquiry about the antenatal yoga which is great and I don't want to lose people when I stop either. I'll need to consider what options I've got.

Wednesday, 25th July

Once again I took the kids to their football kickers session. They seem to really enjoy it and I'm so proud of them, though later on at bedtime they say they don't want to go the next day. After their session, I dropped them off at their gran's for the rest of the day. I had the whole afternoon to myself and with the weather being hot and sunny I would normally have headed to the park for a walk. Not this time, unfortunately! I just feel the pressure of the baby in my pelvis and also the heat wasn't making me feel that good so I just sat in the back garden and feel asleep for a wee while after my lunch. I had a tasty king prawn salad sandwich and yogurt.

Then, I had an appointment to get my bikini line waxed – it was agony. It's not been done properly for a while and it's so much more sensitive when you are pregnant. I worried I might go into labour later today!

Then I went for a swim – I did 60 lengths in my new swimming costume… Which felt pretty tight! But I felt great to be feeling light and I had plenty energy and breath in me. The kids didn't get brought back till after 7pm, so I really did get time to myself… I had a pizza and then got some chocolate and diet coke from the ice-cream van. Like I needed it, but hey, it was a treat.

My legs are now feeling extra jumpy again, my back is hurting as the baby is digging into my ribs and I can feel it right round my back on this side.

Thursday, 26th July

Well, the kids didn't really sleep much longer today despite the later bedtime last night. I got them ready for their football session again and David made it along to watch them in their last 20 minutes. They have seemed really tired today so we didn't do much this afternoon. I headed off for a nap after lunchtime and the kids watched a bit of telly. I swear I set my alarm for 20 minutes and woke up after 15 dreaming that it was morning and I'd slept in for something! I must have been in a really deep sleep, and so quickly, and I felt so refreshed.

We then went to the shops to get some new paint and school stuff for Jane. The kids had a great time painting in the back garden when we got back, and I got on with the tidying up. Both David and my mum arrived about 7pm and David made a brilliant fillet steak and chips dinner. David said it would be his last proper dinner in a few days as he prepares to go away to Amsterdam for this stag weekend. It's going to be 30C there and he's hardly drank much lately at all, never mind a full on session all weekend.

Happy days… I'll try not to worry! Oh, nearly forgot, that's me 33 weeks today and weighing nine stone 9½lbs – just ½ lb off what I was when I was full term with Robbie… As I said, happy days! Also, I used the tens machine on my back, though we weren't quite sure if I should be using it at all! I only had it on at a very low intensity and it did ease up the discomfort. I don't get the back pain every day but when I do the best thing is just to get to bed!

Friday, 27th July

The kids slept till about 7am which was good, I got up and showered first at 6.30am. We left at 7.30am to drop David off for his stag weekend. Me and my Mum got the kids ready and we took them to their last day of their football week.

I went for a swim while my Mum watched the kids. I'm glad I did, what a lovely swim – no lanes but I had three other swimmers compliment me on my swimming technique and suggesting I take up coaching. How lovely!

After lunch and chilling out at home I went to the physio appointment I'd arranged at the maternity hospital. It was pretty good… The physiotherapist did a really through assessment and looked at my alignment, pelvis, foot and back. She also complimented me on my back, saying it was nice to see such a nice back that she could actually find all the right muscles and ribs etc. Two compliments in one day!

I felt pretty reassured that I'm not doing too much wrong and that it's likely my heel pain and everything else is all related, though it's hard to know for sure. She did advise not to do too much balancing yoga postures as this is putting the pelvis under a lot of pressure to rectify the other side. She gave me a support belt for the PSD. It's getting worse and I really need to be careful on the yoga postures where my legs are apart.

After making an omelette and salad for our dinner I headed out for a walk in the forest at the park. I probably walked for 45 minutes and my PSD wasn't too bad… I hope I don't suffer for it tomorrow though. I've really been making the most of having my mum over and I feel so much better for the exercise today.

David even phoned tonight and sounded surprisingly sober – he said he was knackered and ready for bed. The heat has been hard for them all 31ºC and drinking loads.

Well, it's the Olympics ceremony tonight and while I should be getting an early night I'm feeling compelled to watch it. I'm looking forward to watching loads of it on the telly in the next few weeks. I've also just been looking over the details of the girls coming to the antenatal yoga tomorrow morning – there should be four new girls starting, so looking forward to it.

Saturday, 28th July

The kids slept well till after 7am, hooray! I got us all organised and then my sister-in-law came over to watch the kids this morning while I went to my antenatal yoga class. There were eight mums-to-be so I was delighted everyone I expected to see was there.

After the class, I had to take my car to the garage to get the shock absorber fixed – while this was going on I went to Tesco to do the weekly shop. I got soaked on the walk to the supermarket and felt knackered by the time I got home. Meanwhile the kids had been to see Ice Age 4 which they really enjoyed... Especially the pic n mix! The kids made rockets out of water bottles and egg trays and then had a javelin throwing competition to see how far they could throw them. Further inspiration came from watching the gymnastics on the telly this afternoon; I was in the kitchen making dinner and came into the lounge to find the kids jumping off the nestle tables onto the cushions.

David phoned just when the kids were going to bed so had a chance to say, "Night night!" I'm shocked he's even phoning but it's all good.

I've had a magic wee day. I didn't feel much like eating anything big tonight so I just had a chicken and mozzarella toastie with crisps and diet coke. Not maybe my healthiest option. I never normally touch diet coke but I've taken a taste for it during this pregnancy and I'm just going with that.

Sunday, 29th July

I have been absolutely knackered today and feeling pretty groggy, but the show must go on! I look at the date and cannot believe it's nearly August; I thought that the school holidays might drag in and it's just not been the case. It is lovely to not be rushing around in the morning though – I hope the kids don't get a shock when it's time to go back to school and nursery.

The three of us went to the park this morning. My PSD is very much a daily occurrence now and I wore the belt while we walked round the park. We came back to watch the qualifiers for the swimming final 400m females tonight – Rebecca Adlington got through and later got the bronze.

In the afternoon, all inspired by the swimming on the telly, we went swimming! I thought it would be easier on me being in the water, but it's still so tiring doing anything. Then we went to Decathlon to get the kids googles and me some cushioning insoles to help with my right foot. The kids have been pretty well behaved all day and helped with the housework. David will be back around

11.30pm tonight – it's been a quick weekend and I've not really missed him, purely because I'm used to not seeing him, and I'm getting better sleeps!

Tonight I made a chicken and vegetable pasta for dinner and had a few snacks later on. I've not really had an appetite though and I'm more eating out of feeling like I should and to maybe make me feel a bit better. I've had more diet coke today as well which is definitely making me feel worse but at the time I think it's what I want.

It's now 9pm and two hours ago I set out all my painting stuff to do a watercolour picture of some lovely flowers my mum brought – I just can't be bothered though as I get so tired.

Monday, 30th July

David came home last night about 11.30pm and as I woke up he said, 'I've really missed you… you make me feel safe.' I was sort of laughing as I thought he was probably still drunk but he said it again this morning. I don't think I've ever heard him say that. He did, however, stink of garlic and booze so didn't get too much of a cuddle!

Today has been a great day. David had bought the kids big cuddly toys at the airport – a deer and an elephant which they both love! Me and the kids met my dad at the Science Centre. We had so much fun and my Dad just loved seeing the kids so absorbed and focused in the areas that interested them. Robbie was happy to throw balls into a gold toilet and other buckets; Jane enjoyed dancing to the moves on the big screen – she was brilliant. Here's me having been so against getting something like an Xbox and now I'm thinking it might be a good idea to get her doing more dancing moves!

We also bumped into my cousin and her two kids.

We got home about 4pm and did some crafts and nothing much else. We watched a little bit of the Olympics diving. I made meatballs and bolognaise pasta for us all – David came home about 5.30pm too – he knew he was going to have a shorter day after the stag weekend.

I was determined to do some watercolour painting tonight but I only managed to draw the still life of my flowers, well it's a start. I then got engrossed with the Olympics swimming on the telly and chatting to David. I've been feeling pretty uncomfortable tonight with sore kicks from the baby and lots of Braxton hicks too. I'm really a bit worried that this baby is going to arrive very early. I need to find or get another copy of the hypnobirthing CD I used for Robbie and start listening to it every night.

It's just after 10pm and David is fast asleep and I'm going to read my next chapter of Fifty Shades of Grey – so far it's been a bit disappointing.

Tuesday, 31st July

Today turned out to be a busy wee day. So much for taking it easy, though I know my break is coming tomorrow. I took the kids to Summerlee Heritage Centre after Robbie got the scissors and clippers let loose on him at the barbers. The weather was nice and sunny today so I needed to make the most of it and have a picnic at the play park. I felt a bit crappy standing waiting on the tram for the kids for half an hour. We also managed to squeeze in some pottery painting so all in all it was a lot of fun for them. I felt really bad when I had been telling the kids to be careful with their pottery pieces and then I dropped and broke Jane's as we were getting into the car.

When we came home, I had a power nap and then the neighbours and kids came round to play and have dinner. It was all a bit crazy! Macaroni cheese for the kids and salmon salad for us… It was nice to have dinner with someone else though!

Once they left, I had about half an hour to get the kids bathed and into bed before my friend came around. She's always got so much news as she's had such a turbulent and adventurous time since her marriage ended a few years ago. It's always good to catch up on the gossip.

Got to my bed about 10.30pm – baby has been kicking a lot and it's been pretty uncomfortable.

Wednesday, 1st August

Here we go, into August now! This morning was all about getting the kids ready to meet my mum at Kelburn Country Park and leave them for a few days' sleepover. Both, Jane and Robbie have been saying they are going to miss me and Jane especially has been saying that two nights will feel like too long (I think she's overheard me talking to David), but it's nice all the same! It did feel strange leaving the kids for a few days; I instantly feel like a part of me is missing. I am so very lucky. I nearly crashed the car again coming out the country park… That's about the third time in the last few days I've had a near miss.

I felt really rotten this morning with headaches and nausea again so when I got home I went to bed for a wee power nap. I then headed for a swim. Once again, a man in my lane said I was very fast and good at swimming. I think I might try and get some lessons next year to improve my front crawl technique a bit more. I did just short of the 60 lengths before the inflatables took over the pool for the kids.

After swimming, I headed to the shops to try and get some baby things, but I kept hesitating thinking I might be given some of the things I was going to buy. I had a 6-inch subway tuna takeaway for lunch as a wee treat.

The rest of the afternoon I spent relaxing at home and watching Bradley Wiggins win the gold in cycling. Then my neighbour popped in with a moses basket, carrycot and baby clothes so that was a great help.

I've been out a walk at the park too as it's been a nice night – it took a good 45 minutes of slow walking through the trees, but it was just great. I love the forest.

I'm now waiting on David coming home; he said he'd be home before 8pm and we'd have dinner together.

Well we didn't have the night I'd exactly planned for – we had a row within about five minutes of David being home about finances! Oh dear, it was a biggie. Not pleasant, but I guess it might be the first of many, seeing as I'm not making any money and he is under pressure to make money and take money out the business at this stage.

Thursday, 2nd August

Well, I'm now 34 weeks expecting and when I weighed myself I was surprised the scales said nine stone 9lbs –that's confusing but I'm sure it'll change next week. It was really strange waking up and not having the kids running through to me in the morning. I really miss them and the house is so quiet without them.

That said, I took my time getting up this morning; had breakfast and went back to bed and read my book. My mum phoned and I got to speak to the kids this morning which was lovely. Robbie was so much clearer and chatty on the phone than Jane. They had a good time yesterday with a surprise visit from their cousin too.

I went swimming late morning and I signed Robbie up for his first set of swimming lessons. The guy at reception very nicely gave me my swim for free!

This afternoon, I spent a bit of time on the computer and doing my begging and borrowing for baby goods on Facebook. I've done pretty well – a baby car seat, bouncy chair, steriliser, baby bath. Also, we've got loads of baby vouchers for Tesco from the club card so it's not looking too bad.

I had a wee nap… And why not, and then a bit more reading of the Grey book – I can't see what all the fuss is about, but it is an easy read. I went a walk at the park too as it was a nice night, then sat and had a pizza dinner, followed by a can of coke and a packet of revels from the ice-cream van. A bit of a lazy night watching the Olympics again.

Friday, 3rd August

David's alarm went off at 6am so that was my lie-in over. I just read my book for a little while and then did a half hour of yoga. Then I went for a walk and was stopped by another walker who was so nice and complimentary, saying how great I was looking. I'm getting compliments every day at the moment and lapping it up!

I was a wee bit late for my art class at 10 because I was stopped again by these lovely cyclists who I see all the time. Clearly this was the first time they'd seen my baby bump. My art class was a bit disappointing as I feel I ruined my picture, but then this is all part of it – so I was told.

Then I went for my last swim of the week – got in free again which was a bonus, and did another 60 lengths. So today has been a successful day with getting some exercise. I just chilled out till my mum came back with the kids, though she was an hour late and I was imagining all sorts of horrible scary thoughts about why they were so late.

It was so good to see the kids again – they had such a good break at their gran's and it's been really great to get their cuddles again. We all had oven-baked fish, chips and vegetables and then watched more Olympics on the telly… An exciting life.

Saturday, 4th August

Slept all through the night, which is unusual. There were only four at my yoga class today but I knew of at least four cancellations. It was a lovely wee group and there was more chat at the end because there was only a few of us. Apparently, there is to be a baby boom in February – nine months after the release of the Darker Shades of Grey books!'

After lunch, we had a first birthday party to go to… Lots of lovely, filled croissants and cakes! We then went to the in-laws to see all the family. Everyone was saying how well I am looking; I even thought it would be good to get a few pictures taken, but I didn't really like them. My posture is shocking in the pics! Apart from me feeling really itchy all over and pretty big, there's not much else to mention… The Olympics athletics was amazing – watching Jessica Ennis win gold in the heptathalon, Greg Rutherford in long jump and Mo Farah in the 10,000m. I was a bubbling wreck and I can't even blame pregnancy hormones for this one.

Sunday, 5th August

Well, I just had to watch the highlights from last night all over again and explain it all to Jane – I felt the emotion welling up in my eyes again! Today was a home day as the week ahead is busy enough. I did a massive ironing this morning and then headed to the park with the kids. I was all organised with lots of sports games we could play and then we bumped into their friends at the park. They were happy enough to just stay at the park and then we walked round the park with them on their scooters.

Andy Murray was on the telly so we saw him win Olympic gold in the singles. At long last, and yes, I had another tear in my eye. I set up the sports games in the lounge for the kids while the telly was on. They make up their own games too… always giving me more ideas for my circuits classes! I have felt really lousy all afternoon, a horrible sicky headache that would not shift no matter how much water I drank. I had a really healthy dinner tonight of salad with tuna, egg, spinach and almonds (and of course salad cream), followed by one of my Mum's crispy cakes!

The headache is horrible though and I'm just about to head to bed for a lie down and to listen to the hypnobirthing CD for the first time this pregnancy. My PSD has been especially bad in the second half of the day – a real burning sensation in my pubic bone. I think it's finally starting to dawn on me that the arrival of baby number three and mayhem is really not far away. David has been out all day working and won't be back till after 10pm.

Well I put on the hypnobirthing CD and it really wasn't quite as I remember it. The first difference was that it was aimed at both you and your partner, second it just seemed to be repeating itself constantly. I know I did fall asleep but it was still going on longer than what it should have. I'll need to listen to it again; from my memory of it before there were a lot of positive affirmations repeated but on this one there weren't any. This and the rainbow relaxation are the bits I was hoping to listen to in the hospital again. I woke up about 9.30pm with it still going on. I decided to eat a few packets of crisps and drink some flat coke! Feeling rough. I watched Usain Bolt win his Olympic title again for the 800m then went to sleep.

Monday, 6th August

I've not had a good day, but on reflection, I suppose I've had so many good days I was due at least one bad one. I have felt so tired and grumpy today and it really rubbed off on the kids. My head has been sore all day, despite keeping sipping drinks and my tummy itchy. My legs have been so restless that at one point I had to lie on the floor with my back propped by cushions and legs up on the couch while I read a story to the kids. I was like a nodding dog trying to read stories to them and had to have a nap in the afternoon.

I really could just have stayed in bed all day today… Given half the chance! The one good thing was Robbie started his swimming lessons this morning and I just felt so proud of him. He was doing as he was told and seemed to enjoy it. Jane has seemed really whiny today, maybe it's been no more than normal but because of how I've felt we really didn't get on too well. Had a bit of moment with her where I got really angry over something, probably well out of proportion. Sometimes it would be nice to just walk away and go and lie in my bed when she is having tantrums. I know I added fuel to the fire though and I felt really bad about it and did say sorry.

I'm just waiting on David coming home about 7.30pm and he said he'd make dinner. I'm still feeling pretty low in mood today, not feeling much up to talking to anyone and just wanting to go to bed. I think deep inside I'm starting to get a bit anxious about birth and beyond and how close it all seems now.

We had a lovely chicken stir-fry dinner and David had his good listening ears on and was a bit of a shoulder to cry on.

Tuesday, 7th August

Today was a surprise sunny day. After having to drop off David's forgotten PC at his work we went to Kelvingrove Park to meet a friend and her two girls. Had a great day with the kids and their friends; did a fair wee bit of walking while they were on their scooters. Enjoyed a decaf soya cappuccino and some carrot cake for my lunch.

Got home and had a turkey breast roll and sat out the back with the kids. Still reading this Fifty Shades book – it's OK, though definitely not a book I can't put down, but I might as well finish it now.

For dinner, it was salmon salad for me tonight, followed by a FAB ice-lolly and then later strawberries and melon. My neighbour popped round to ask us to a BBQ and couldn't believe the size of my bump, saying, 'Are you sure it's not twins?' Thanks.

Pretty much nothing else happening. I still had the headaches and nausea in the morning though my pelvic pain was better today even though I was standing a lot of the day. I feel pretty uncomfortable tonight with a sore back and restless legs and really plan to have an earlier night.

Wednesday, 8th August

My cousin arrived today with her kids and the sun has been shining hot, hot, hot all day! I have been overheating like no man's business. All that fits me now are my black leggings and they are too tight round my hips (rolled down). Although I haven't done much today, it's still been non-stop with the kids and all their demands – paddling pool, drinks, ice-lollies, read me this… It goes on.

We all had some rolls for lunch and ice-lollies, loads of juice and then strawberries. Our food supplies seem to have disappeared really quickly this week… the fridge is almost bare.

I have felt MASSIVE today, maybe my tummy is swollen but I just feel I can hardly move. Trying to pick all the kids' things off the ground and floor is physically quite hard work and my back is hurting tonight as a result.

I never really picked up much of an appetite tonight and decided to have just half of my piece of salmon and some cous cous salad mix. Also had a piece of David's haggis pizza when he came in at 9pm. I'm heading to bed pretty soon now… I really miss the getting out to the park in the evening, even just for a walk. It was such a beautiful night… Instead I have become a beach whaled couch potato!

Thursday, 9th August

I am 35 weeks and weighing nine stone 11½ lbs – 2½lbs heavier than last week, though last weeks seemed to be a bit of a blip!

It's been another scorcher of a day. Another morning of meeting friends and children at the park. After lunch, we went to the shops as I needed to get a birthday pressie for a nephew and I also really needed to buy some shorts and cooler clothes before I spontaneously combust. I had two ice-lollies today and lots of water to try and keep cool. The kids' paddling pool was pretty refreshing too.

I bumped into a client at the shops (she's also expecting) – I felt huge and although she's 20 weeks she's not really got a bump yet.

Although I'm not exercising per se, I've still been on the go and on my feet most of the day. My back is sore in the usual place it gets sore… Down the right side and my feet are understandably feeling pretty hot and swollen.

David is home tonight and although it's after 8.30pm, and we've not eaten yet, it's still nice to have him home. I've not got a great deal of an appetite these days and find I am eating plenty little snacks every few hours. We're having prawn and vegetable stir-fry hopefully with noodles. David's also bought me a piece of carrot cake which I will savour!

Friday, 10th August

Today the kids were going to their cousin's birthday party – it was in a soft play with all their other cousins. My mother-in-law came to pick them up which was really good of her and this gave me a few hours in the morning to go for a swim and have some me time.

The heat is really tiring me out. After my swim, I came home and had scrambled egg roll for lunch followed by my delicious carrot cake. I sat out the back for less than half an hour and found the heat unbearable – the cold leather couch was a welcome relief! I've had my new shorts on today and decided to put some instant fake tan on my legs as they are so peely wally. Well I needn't have bothered! When I went to get the kids at my mother-in-law's they were all playing with their water pistols and soaking everyone… Fake tan dribbling and streaky legs result, a lovely look!

It was great to see all the cousins together and Jane and Robbie have had a great day. Well, tonight I took Jane to her swimming lesson and I thought I might pass out with the heat in the swimming pool. I bumped into my friend on the way out with her girls and again she commented on how I looked bigger today. I am getting a bit fed up with this now, constant conflicting opinions. My sisters-in-law were lovely with their comments saying how well I looked. I think the family are sure we are having another girl… because of the way I'm carrying the baby. I'm struggling to remember how I carried Jane let alone how everyone else remembers.

I've not felt much like eating a dinner tonight and have just been nibbling again on oatcakes, banana and toast. Heartburn has been bad today again and the double strength Gaviscon that the chemist gave me is so thick and disgusting. I ought to go now as I realise all I'm doing is complaining.

Saturday, 11th August

I took the chance to go for a walk this morning at the park – beautiful day and I felt like I could walk really well this morning. Bumped into friends out walking and jogging so it was lovely to have a wee catch up. Next was my antenatal yoga class and it was great to see seven turn up today. Everyone seems to be really getting to know each other and have a chat so that makes me feel like I'm doing my job right. I've passed all their email addresses round each other and hope we can all keep in touch, especially for some post-natal fitness classes.

After lunch, (tuna salad and oatcakes for me) we all went up the street with the kids on bikes and scooters – my walking pace was a bit faster than comfortable and we were out for probably about 45 minutes. My inner thighs are feeling the strain and I'm feeling a bit weak. My heartburn has been relentless all day today, despite using the extra strength Gaviscon.

We were to have a BBQ today but it was only when everything was ready that David remembered that the BBQ is broken! So it all got made in the kitchen. It was really lovely to just spend the day together, the four of us.

I had David take a picture of me as I feel there isn't any really showing my baby bump, and since this WILL be the last time I am pregnant, I'd like to have a memory of it! Wee Robbie wanted in on the picture so it turned out to be a really nice and natural picture of us.

Tonight's Olympics (what am I going to do once it's over tomorrow!) was Mo Farah winning gold in the 5000m.

Sunday, 12th August

I have such great kids… I managed to stay in bed relaxing and watching a bit of telly this morning till 9am. That was with David away at work by 7.30am… The kids just accepted I was staying in bed a bit longer and were drawing pictures and entertaining themselves.

We had a nice slow start but when we did get ready we went to the park with the scooters, and then bumped into their friends. We spent a bit of time playing at the park too and then came home for lunch. I don't know what's wrong with me today, but I just didn't feel much like salad and instead had a banana and cheese toastie, followed by a cookie. I didn't even have a proper dinner tonight, I just couldn't face the salmon and had no appetite.

After the kids were in bed, I had a bath and then had a fab ice-lolly followed by a bowl of rice crispies. I'm sitting in front of the telly, probably for the last night, watching the closing ceremony of the Olympics. I had a good chat with my dad, once again about the Olympics, sport and children. Oh, and the problem with McDonald's fast food chains and kids diets in this country!

Monday, 13th August

I'm writing this on Tuesday night so already my memory of what I did yesterday is fading. Robbie had his swimming lesson in the morning and then we had a quick check in at Clark's shoes shop for Jane's gym shoes. It was a pretty quiet day really, a visit to the park and dinner, that was about it.

The main issue I remember was my pal getting in touch about the school run arrangements. I assumed that everyone would be doing their own thing this week for the start of school, especially since their daughter has not been adjusting too well to going to school in the mornings. I know we hadn't sat down and made a clear plan this year but I had made suggestions that I wasn't likely to be much help when our baby arrives and that I had applied even for a place on the bus for Jane (though not heard anything yet). I'd hinted I wasn't too happy about the car seat arrangements and putting one of the kids in the front, even for a short journey. Oh hell, texting is not the best way to be having this conversation.

David came home for 6pm tonight and I got to go to my art class – I really enjoyed it and managed to finish my watercolour picture. Now on to the oil painting portrait – it took me a while to decide on what I'd like to do.

I didn't really have much to eat since lunch time today – really off my food today. I did have a drifter bar as a snack and then a banana and single cream when I came in from my art class.

Tuesday, 14th August

We made some fairy cakes this morning as the neighbours were coming round to play. It was pretty loud and mad in the house; I felt bad about not asking our other friend round; I just don't think I could've coped having seven children and trying to have a conversation. I did pretty much say this to my neighbour about the school run and looking after three of my own children and having the others on top of this – I'm not quite sure how I'd cope with it!

The weather today was pretty crazy – really hot and then torrential rain. My washing came in tonight almost dry despite having been soaked many times. Me and Jane got stuck in with the "nesting" today too – we blitzed the spare (baby) room – clearing all the shelves and tidying up the kids' room. I was starting to get pretty cranky with Jane though for no real reason, just that she wanted me to do more and more with her (understandable!); Robbie just drew pictures downstairs. I do feel like I'm getting somewhere now, though still not done anything about my hospital bag!

The afternoon just disappeared doing all this and before I knew it it was dinner time. I made us all a simple pasta dish which went down pretty well. David will be in about 9pm tonight so I'll just chill out as much as I can!

Later… Well, I've managed to find the original playlist from my hypnobirthing – affirmations and the rainbow relaxation, so I'm well chuffed. I listened to it and it is really good; so relaxing and will take me back to a time when I birthed comfortably and naturally with Robbie. David hasn't come home at 9pm… Wonder when he will be in?

Wednesday, 15th August

Well, what a rough night's sleep I had. David didn't come home till after 11pm and I just couldn't get to sleep… Not sure if it was partly because I had done the relaxation CD earlier or that I was annoyed about David. I was up several times during the night too and just couldn't switch off. Robbie was up early, just after 6am and Jane slept till well after 7am.

I've been trying to get them a little bit more prepared for the school run tomorrow by getting them ready earlier, so today was no different. We then went to Morrisons to get some food essentials but also essentials for my hospital bag. Think it's about time I did something about it!

David's mum picked the kids up about 11.30am to give me a break, and I was just so tired I decided to go for a nap after an early lunch. It's been another warm though windy day and so I just couldn't face going swimming and instead opted for the park. I managed a walk of about an hour through the forest which

I loved. People are looking at me though as if to question whether I should be walking on my own through the woods in my condition!

I then went to Mothercare and got measured for nursing bras. Spent another £60 on bras. I had a "picnic" chocolate bar before going to pick up the kids from their gran's. Another afternoon of soft play, goodies and TV. Jane had a bit of a bad attitude on her when I asked her to get ready and wouldn't say goodbye to her gran or help carry the bag. I was shocked – maybe this is her just gearing up for school tomorrow ... Bringing back the cheek and tantrums, I hope not!

We just had a light dinner of a chicken roll and salad followed by a yogurt. David has said he will be in not long after 8pm tonight so we'll see. I've just listened to the affirmations again on the CD and will leave the second part to bedtime. Now on to the second book in the Darker Shades of Grey trilogy. I'm shattered though and my heartburn has been terrible today. Not helped I suppose by the tomatoes and pesto pasta I had at lunchtime. Also been drinking a pink lemonade drink, so it's all making it worse.

Thursday, 16th August

Today was Jane's first day back at school and Robbie back at nursery in the afternoon too. All went well, though my forgetful baby brain is taking over – I went back to the school playground and the office to search for my bag that I thought I'd taken out with me… Only to find it still at home.

I am 36 weeks today and weighed myself to find I was similar to last week – nine stone 11 ¾lbs. I felt really uncomfortable today, especially when I went walking round the park with Robbie on his scooter. The pace was too fast for me and by the end of the walk I had to stop and go really slow as the pelvic pain was too intense – burning and jabbing pains. I had a bit of a break once we got to the play park.

After taking Robbie to nursery, I went for a swim in the pool – I did another 60 lengths. I feel comfortable swimming however I am really getting a lot of stares from people now. I don't remember people being quite as obvious about it before.

It was then time to pick up Jane and Robbie – they'd got on fine, no problems on first day back… Relief. As the afternoon wore on though my mood got a bit grumpy and low – I really feel like my energy levels and tolerance get so low as the day goes on. David came in about 5.30pm tonight to spend some time with the kids after their first day back. I just wanted to sit about and do nothing – I had really been looking forward to him coming home, and it reminded me that this is actually what it's like for most families. I'm getting a little anxious at the thought of how much work it's going to be early on when I've got the three of them and little help from David.

I had a chat with my mum tonight and although she has offered her help, I'm not really sure how much I want someone coming and staying with me. I don't want people around when I'm feeling tired and teary. I think I'd rather just have someone take away my ironing and do some cleaning. Maybe for them to look after Jane and Robbie from time to time, away from the house, just to give me some space and rest.

David made a lovely pasta bolognaise tonight which I enjoyed more than I thought I would. I followed this with some strawberries and cream and a kit-kat! I'm heading off to bed now, as David gets stuck into his tax return work.

Friday, 17th August

Today was my midwife appointment – it all went well, our baby is in the right position with its head down, in fact, its head is on the brim of my pelvic bowl and this is why I feel so much discomfort at the moment. Apparently, the baby can move back up and down from here until onset of labour and the baby's head may not get engaged until labour with a second/third pregnancy.

I've been getting frequent tightenings, just like a dull period pain all day today. I think that this baby is going to arrive quite soon. I had hoped to relax at a soft play with Robbie this morning but it was closed so I went to Starbucks for a wee treat of my decaf soya caramel machiatta and a skinny blueberry muffin.

After dropping Robbie off at nursery, I went a walk through the forest again. I felt not too bad and bumped into one of my clients, who clearly thought I was looking pretty big. I walked for about an hour though it was really clammy today. Then I picked up Jane and had some one-to-one time with her – doing some painting and then again relaxing with a little TV.

We all went to Jane's swimming lesson tonight and Robbie and I went in for a swim as the reception area was just too warm to bear last week. Well, the pool and changing area was filthy and stinky and I really need to complain. We did have a good time in the pool though and bumped into friends.

David was home by the time we got home at 6.30pm which was lovely. After the kids were in bed we got a Chinese takeaway. This is the first I've had in years. I just had chicken fried rice though I did eat far too much. With our baby positioned so low down I really feel uncomfortable with any clothes on, even maternity clothes. So I was sitting again just in my underwear eating dinner! I then did a bit of research for my antenatal class tomorrow morning and I'm going to head to bed now… Just before 10pm. I am shattered.

Saturday, 18th August

I loved my antenatal yoga class this morning – there was another good turnout of eight mums-to-be, including a mum who is 40 weeks and another that is 38 weeks! It feels so good to be taking this class and hopefully making a little difference to the girls as they prepare for labour. I then went for a walk around the park – I only went once around and my PSD was pretty evident. My pace was slow, but I'm not giving up. I'd rather suffer a little bit of pain than put my feet up all day… Not that that's an option anyway!

When I got back, the rest of the family were already home with the shopping. Friends came over this afternoon and David made steak for dinner, followed by a chocolate tart with raspberries and cream… Delicious! It was a great afternoon and they stayed till nearly midnight. They were a reminder as to how lucky we are to have conceived three children so easily and to have been so blessed with healthy and happy children, since they are needing to get help to conceive. Jane was a little strange though which was unusual; she seemed pretty sensitive and was talking in a baby voice. Robbie was extra confident and stealing the show.

Sunday, 19th August

I managed to stay in bed till about 8.30am though I was reading to the kids for a wee while. They both slept till 7.30am which was also great! We've just had a lazy day at home today; I shouldn't say lazy since I cleaned all morning from the night before… Dishes, washings, putting away clothes, cleaning floors. I was knackered and after my lunch (banana and cheese toastie) I had a sleep while the kids watched telly.

After telly, I read to the kids again for another 45 minutes until I could take no more of my twitchy restless legs. The kids went out to play on the street but it wasn't long before the older kids in the street were down playing with them. I'm getting really sick of telling them to play with kids their own age – I wouldn't mind so much if they weren't so cheeky and also I can't stand the way they teach my kids nothing about road safety. The final straw was when Robbie had a nasty fall and skint his knees. I told the girls that they weren't setting a good example and to play with children their own age…again. I was raging… Fully expect I might get one of their parents knocking on my door to complain!

A little painting session with the kids later seemed to help ease Robbie's pain… He's always so brave too. Today I've continued to have period pains frequently but I'm trying not to attach too much to this as I suppose it could go on for a good number of weeks!

David is to be in later, about 9pm, so I'll likely have an egg salad tonight and an early night with my book.

Well, I did some yoga to my rainbow relaxation CD – it was lovely and really helped with the breathing. David stuck to his word and was in by 9pm.

Monday, 20th August

Another week has begun and the school run is upon us! Robbie had his swimming lesson this morning and I had a quick swim too – I only managed 46 lengths in that time but it was good to not be going back again this afternoon. Robbie is fascinated with my "boobies" at the moment and couldn't resist telling me in the swimming cubicle that he liked my "boobies"! He wasn't quiet about it either… Mortified!

It's been so easy going this morning with him… After lunch I had a wee nap and nearly never woke up on time for his nursery!

After dropping Robbie off, I went a walk twice round the park – it was a slow walk but I'm pleased I managed it without too much pain. I just want to keep as active as possible. When I came home though, I fell asleep again and just didn't want to move from the couch. Luckily, my friend was picking up Jane and that meant I didn't have two runs to school and then nursery to get Robbie.

The kids have been great this afternoon. Jane hasn't been given any real homework yet (a total contrast to what she got this time last year) and she was still okay with doing a few sentences about her day after dinner. Her behaviour has been fantastic so far.

I don't think I'll be eating much for tea either tonight… I had a kit-kat chunky earlier but I've just not got much of an appetite. Think it'll be oatcakes and banana. Might have a bath tonight too and listen to my hypnobirthing CD. I must get my bag packed, though the tightening's have eased off today.

Tuesday, 21st August

A visit to the soft play this morning with two other mums – proved more relaxing than I thought it was going to be! After dropping Robbie at nursery, I went a walk at park, through the forest. It's maybe not what most pregnant people would choose to do at this stage of their pregnancy, as I later found out when I was telling the mums at the school run. I'm not frightened of the forest or being on my own in the forest – I just love the trees and nature more than anything. I walked for about 30 minutes, came home and then had a wee 15-minute power nap before picking up Jane and Robbie.

Once again, their behaviour has been really good – Jane did her homework without too much reluctance and we all had a good tea of pizza and salad, followed by an ice-lolly. One bath later and bed and then the night is all mine.

Listened to my birthing affirmations' on the hypnobirthing CD and then watched the countdown to the Paralympics – It's so inspiring and I'm really looking forward to watching it.

The tightenings have returned a bit more this evening. My neighbour gave me her leftover raspberry leaf teabags today – I'd kind of decided I wasn't going to bother taking them this time but since she has given me them I might try a few a day. Fruit intake has been pineapple and apple, not much else but a bit of salad with dinner was good. Still needing to take the Gaviscon but only when I have highly acidic foods. I bought some empire biscuits today and nearly demolished two… I just kept thinking about them all day and decided I had to buy them.

I'm sitting here just now and my legs are so twitchy that I could jump through the ceiling! Heading for bed with my Mr Grey book… Still reading it!

Wednesday, 22nd August

Went a walk round park with Robbie on his scooter – every day I'm so grateful for our little time together in the morning. He's such great company and constantly telling me how much he loves me and that I'm the best mum in the world! My pace was pretty slow with this baby bearing down on me.

We didn't do much till nursery time, I had a banana roll for lunch and some toast. It's not been a very nutritious day for me – white bread and then at dinner time I had instant noodles! I'm even embarrassed thinking about it… I haven't eaten instant noodles since I was a student. I suppose at least I've had some fruit today – strawberries, melon and apple, but it's not enough. Had another ice-lolly tonight too.

At least I've done some exercise with the walking and then swimming with one of the girls from my antenatal yoga class. I didn't do my usual number of lengths but spent a good bit of time chatting which was lovely.

Sitting tonight, I'm feeling so uncomfortable, both with the size of my bump and the dull period pains I've been getting a lot of today. I'm thinking I ought to just get to bed though I've started watching a film Little Miss Sunshine. It's pretty funny. David's not planning on being in till about 11pm again tonight – I don't know how he does it, working for 15 hours a day pretty much on his own.

Right, bed for me – my legs are so twitchy, ggrrrr…

Thursday, 23rd August

37 weeks today – can hardly believe it! Weight is at nine stone 13 and a bit lbs… Not long to go now! I had a bit of an easy day but the evening seemed to make up for it. This morning Robbie was away at gymnastics with his friend so I had the morning to myself. What did I do? Another swim and did my usual 60 lengths, though it took me a lot longer than normal, even though I felt just the same.

When Robbie came back we just had an hour together before he was off to nursery. I had salmon and potatoes and some salad at lunch time as I really don't feel like eating much in the evenings, or that should say, eating much healthy stuff!

While he was in nursery I came home and actually put my feet up, read for a while and then listened to my hypnobirthing CD till I picked up Jane. The antics came when homework was mentioned and Jane was up to last year's tricks and refusing to do it; being cheeky and saying she wasn't bothered about being in her bedroom. She eventually came out the room with her homework done but she missed a lovely time outside playing in the good weather.

We all had a good dinner and the rest of the date and cinnamon cake I'd made last night. But when it came to getting Robbie to help tidy or get ready for his bath, he was constantly ignoring me. I normally can placate him and manage to get him to do whatever it is, but my patience was fraught and I felt I wasn't being as strict with him as with Jane. So this time, Robbie was given a right telling off and no telly while his sister saw a little before bedtime. He was so upset, the most I've ever seen him, but maybe he will help a bit more. I found it really upsetting seeing him so upset too. Oh dear, I'll be glad when they are in bed sleeping.

I've done quite a bit of housework tonight and got back on top of the ironing. I've got a bit of pelvic pain and usual dull period pain. I'm going to bed soon – 10pm... David doesn't expect to be in till midnight; he's hoping to meet deadlines and then take the weekend off.

Friday, 24th August

I didn't get a good night sleep at all... In fact not many of them are. I woke at 11.30pm and then 12.30pm when David came in, then twice again a couple of hours later. Robbie was then up at 6am at the toilet, though he was sent back to bed, he came in again nearer 7am for a cuddle. I've been having these tightening's again – at least I seem much more aware of them, especially if I wake up during the night or first thing in the morning.

A walk round the park this morning with Robbie and some friends and I was knackered. I came home and had some cheese on toast for my lunch and then fell asleep while Robbie watched the telly.

It's been a pretty relaxing day though as I had a wee spa treatment. I had a 30-minute back massage, which I wouldn't be surprised if it actually brought on labour! It was pretty hard and a bit sore, which I never thought it would be during pregnancy. The facial was lovely and was done with me sitting up. I then had a wee cup of raspberry and strawberry tea with my little scone, cream and strawberry jam. When I came home everyone was still out so I had the chance to listen to my CD again. David picked the kids up and took Jane to her swimming lesson and Robbie in swimming with him. I actually feel so uncomfortable, sore and itchy wearing clothes that I just want to go into labour in the next week.

I had salmon in a roll for tea and now David has just brought through some spare oven chips he's made! I'm going for a bath and an early night.

Saturday, 25th August

What a night I had. I was up at the toilet about 2.30am and then at 4am was woken with sudden back pain in my lower right back. I really thought this is it, I'm starting labour now. I got up to move around and the pain lasted no more than maybe two-three minutes but it was a horrible reminder to Jane's labour and how intense the pain can suddenly be. Once the pain subsided I started to think, *Bring it on, bring on the pain and getting closer to birth!*

Well I couldn't really get back to sleep and then wee Robbie was up at 5am and I never really settled again; with every wee twinge I'd think I was maybe going to be having a baby this weekend.

Other thoughts were that I'd need to cancel the antenatal yoga this morning. Well, suffice to say, I didn't cancel my yoga and once I was up and moving around I felt pretty much back to normal, although my back has been uncomfortable all day. I really think the massage yesterday has done something to hurt my back and hopefully it will settle down again.

The yoga class was really good, another great turnout of seven "students". I am going to miss this class so much. I think I've managed to get another teacher to take over the class so I'm really happy about that, although the majority of the class are 35 weeks plus. One of the girls is 42 weeks on Tuesday and getting so frustrated to still be waiting.

The rest of the day we had family over for lunch. We went to Kelvingrove Park and the kids had a ball, I managed to keep on my feet most of the time. I've felt like I've been constipated all day and I've tried to keep drinking loads of water but it's just not working. I had a lovely lie down in bed to help with the back pain and it was so lovely having David around to help with making dinner for the kids.

Later David and I had a chicken and bacon salad for dinner and then I had some carrot cake later. David has offered me his boxer shorts to wear as I can't even wear my PJs without feeling like everything is digging into me.

Sunday, 26th August

Well, today was to be my long lie-in morning since David was taking the day off for us to get better organised. I slept better too, not waking till about 5.30am for the toilet. I didn't really get back to sleep after 6.30am when Robbie came in but I was still getting a rest as David got up with the kids at 7am. Read for a little while in bed then got ready for about 9am.

David took the kids to mass while I went a walk for around 30 mins. My PSD was a little sore at the start but I felt much better by the end of the walk; I also listened to my hypnobirthing affirmations as I walked which was good. The back pain had really eased off this morning however by the end of the day it was pretty uncomfortable again.

We've had a good family day, kids had some play with friends and David got right into organising the spare room and moving the double bed around. I'm starting to feel more ready and prepared for our baby arriving… I could even say excited. There has been a lot less movement by our baby today though and I'm trying not to worry about it. I'm going to head to bed by 9pm as I'm so itchy wearing clothes and feeling knackered.

I've eaten far too much rubbish today – a donut, carrot cake and ice-cream! What's that all about! Probably a reason for feeling pretty crap tonight. We had meatballs and spaghetti for dinner tonight and it was delicious – it's pretty difficult eating that at the table and getting close enough (due to size of baby bump!) and to not dribble it all down me. David has been teaching the kids a new song – "Donald where's your troosers" – it's been hilarious watching them singing it.

Monday, 27th August

I had a horrible night's sleep again – up several times and then at 5.30am I was lying in bed awake and thinking about how little movement I'd felt over the last few days. I managed to get myself into a panic and all the possible outcomes were really terrifying. I started moving around to try and get some movement – I did get a little movement but it just feels so much softer and subtle than normal. I was almost thinking I would need to phone the hospital and go and get checked. So, a tired start to the day.

Jane was up first about 6.45am and got a telling off for waking up Robbie too. I left David to get the kids' breakfast as I really feel he needs to realise that this is what he'll be doing when our baby arrives. I asked him to make Jane's lunch too and I didn't get a good response… Not sure how he's going to cope with the changes I'm expecting in the morning.

After Jane's school run, Robbie and I went to his swimming lesson and I fitted in a good wee swim. I was swithering whether to still go for a swim; the option of sitting in the really stuffy waiting room or risking feeling worse than I do (I've got a cold at the moment). I decided I had to go for a swim and make the most of my time alone.

Robbie was hilarious in the changing rooms again. Today he was squeezing his nipples and asking what they were. Then he asked if I had any (I was standing without my top on, I thought it was obvious!). Then he wanted to know what they were for and I quietly tried to explain that mine will be feeding the baby when it arrives. I feel I'm giving him a biology lesson every time we go swimming!

After dropping Robbie off at nursery, I went to get my bikini line waxed – this was agony again and lying on my back, although not totally flat, wasn't very comfortable either. But it's done and I don't know when I'll get the chance to get it done again. Then it was straight back to school to pick up Jane. I decided it would be nice to get some one-to-one time together before picking up Robbie. Jeez, the nightmare of homework and a Jane that just hasn't got the interest to try sometimes. The homework should only have taken 10 minutes maximum, though this went on all night with her refusing to try and sound out words, crying every time she got something wrong. Oh dear, I didn't have much patience left and put the two of them to bed before even 7pm.

I've sat now and had my dinner, tidied up the dishes and hoovered. It's taking all my effort though as my lower back is really sore and my inner right thigh feels sore and weak. The baby is moving a good bit more though which is reassuring and I'm just generally feeling the pain of the pressure on my pelvis. I've been using my swiss ball to sit on more now and hope to use this in labour.

I later phoned my sister for a catch up as I thought if I don't do it now I'll unlikely fit it in at all. I'm not a big fan of sitting on the phone all night, and the line was pretty poor, but we did chat for about an hour which was good. David came home around 9.30pm so not too late after all.

Tuesday, 28th August

Well this was the date that had somehow resonated with me as a due date, but it doesn't look anywhere likely! Had a terrible night's sleep again… This has become a habit reporting on my sleep, but I swear I saw every hour on the clock last night. I don't even know what has been waking me up since it's not the toilet or our baby kicking. I am, however, loaded with the cold and my breathing is pretty stuffy during the night… Maybe that's it.

I'm having some crazy, crazy dreams. One I remember was that Robbie was getting spoilt rotten by his dad and being allowed to play till late at night, get up during the night, and being given ice-cream and whatever else he wanted. In the dream he was behaving quite badly and his dad wouldn't bother telling him off, meanwhile his sister was getting a raw deal. Funnily enough, it was just after having this dream that wee Robbie came into our room at about 4.30am – I had to really take a moment to remind myself that I had just had a dream and it wasn't real life!

I'm definitely feeling a bit on edge and the lack of sleep is probably not helping. After the school run, I took Robbie to football training with his friend.

On the way home from football, I heard great news about one of the antenatal yoga mums and the birth of her son during the night. I love hearing all the good news and it's like a celebration every time to hear of someone else's joy.

After getting the kids from school/nursery, I'd hoped to go to the shops to get some cards and more leggings for my expanding tummy (I just can't get comfortable at all). Jane managed to change these plans with her automatic refusal to try and do some homework while waiting on Robbie's nursery finishing. I don't know what has changed since last week when she found it all pretty straight-forward. I decided to text David and he came home for a few hours. She was really upset and being extremely difficult but it made such a difference to me to have the help. I just went to the shops with Robbie. I didn't manage any exercise today even though weather was pretty nice when the kids were away. The strain on my pubic bone and pelvis is just too great and I was so tired from last night I thought it would be best if I just had a sleep. I hope I'm feeling better tomorrow and more like a swim again.

David went back to work again tonight at 7pm and I am so grateful of him picking up on the need for him to be at home for a few hours tonight. We had chicken tikka and rice dinner and I followed this with some ice-cream and some biscuits! I'm well and truly getting the sweet food in now! I'm going to head up to bed now – it's just 8.30pm and going to watch The Midwives in bed!

Wednesday, 29th August

A slightly better sleep last night – David didn't get in till 11.30pm and I was up at the toilet twice and I couldn't get back to sleep for a while. I went a walk with friends after the school run and then back home for a coffee. Robbie was so well behaved and we were all able to have a proper chat. He was playing well with my friends baby which was lovely to see. I can't quite believe that we are actually going to have another baby in the house soon… Very soon.

I was shattered after a light lunch and had a wee nap while Robbie was watching telly. I'm still loaded with the cold and so avoided a swim and instead took a really slow walk (through the forest) while listening to my hypnobirthing CD affirmations. Once home, I dyed my hair (it was getting so grey) and then cleaned the shower… Which was really difficult to do. I picked up Jane from my friend's house and then Robbie from nursery. I've had a much better night with

Jane – she did her number homework and story without any fuss. We all ate dinner together – I had salmon and Moroccan cous cous and now I'm thinking about what else I can have!

David is going to the football tonight with his pal so he'll be in later again. I've started to watch the Paralympic opening ceremony on the telly – I just can't help but think there is no need for these over-the-top ceremonies that cost the earth. I'd rather hear all about the Paralympians and their sports.

Thursday, 30th August

I'm 38 weeks today and feeling every bit of it. I weighed myself and surprisingly was just about ½lb heavier than last week, so still sitting just under the 10 stone mark. I had another easy enough day today as my friend's parents once again took Robbie for the morning to a soft play with his pal. I did go a slow walk round the park but this time stuck to the loch side and went round twice. It was a lovely morning though a bit nippy and my cold is still well set in me. I've had splitting sore headaches around my eyes and really gritty eyes so the break from the kids has been welcome.

I had more rest this afternoon when Robbie went to nursery for a few hours. I had another short nap, as so tired. David came home about 6pm and I got ready for my little night out with friends – two unfortunately had to cancel, so four of us went to the casino for a special dinner and then had a wee hustle ourselves.

I had a delicious duck pate to start with and then seabass followed by a lemon tart and raspberry sorbet. It was all so tasty and I surprised myself how much I could fit in! I also had two small glasses of red wine, which is a first for me during any pregnancy, but I just thought that it wouldn't do any harm at this late stage. They went down a treat, though I felt a wee bit uncomfortable ordering them when no-one else was having one and I'm sitting there heavily pregnant!

Once again, I was lucky enough to pick a winner on my first go of the roulette and won £35. When we left my winnings had paid for my dinner and the £10 bet with £2 extra!

Friday, 31st August

I really am getting fed up with being pregnant and I don't think I ever got to a point where I said that before. My sleeping is rubbish and I feel so uncomfortable. The pain in my pubic area has worsened and I have hardly been up to walking at all today. Since we all (except David) have bad colds, I just stayed in this morning with Robbie and read books and drew pictures. I had a midwife appointment which went fine though she did say she thought I'd grown well over the last few weeks, and the baby is going to be bigger than my other two; also that the baby has nudged down further still. I've to see her again next week.

Robbie is at nursery just now as I catch up with this journal.

Our other friend's mum is very ill in hospital and we don't think she is going to make it much longer. Another client/friend lost her Mum yesterday morning to cancer too, it's so devastating.

I've asked David to pick up Robbie and let me have a total rest off my feet and see if this pain eases off. I took Jane to her swimming lesson and decided that despite my cold I would have a swim. I felt much better for it as it is time off my feet and I don't have any discomfort when swimming.

We had a fairly early night, well I did as my legs were so twitchy and I'm so uncomfortable sitting on the couch. David did give me a nice little leg and baby bump rub though!

Saturday, 1st September

Oh well, my grand plans of having our baby in August have been blown away! It looks like this baby is going to be joining Robbie in the month of September birthdays. Poor wee Robbie is loaded with the cold today and constantly grunting.

I took my last antenatal yoga class for a few months – there were only five girls there but I've just so enjoyed this class and experiencing the same as what they are going through. A few great stories today – one about a girl who had her baby in the car park on all fours at the infirmary, an hour after her waters broke! Another girl in the class took a day off work to wait on nursery furniture being delivered only for it to come at the end of the day and the guy refused to bring it up the stairs as he was on his own! He actually expected an 8-month-pregnant women to help him… Unbelievable.

We didn't do too much this afternoon but the day disappeared so quickly. I love sitting having lunch on a Saturday with us all sitting round the table. We later went to the park and that was about it. David went to the second leg of his pal's stag do, though he isn't drinking. I've sat and eaten a big cheesy crusty pizza and maltesers while watching the Paralympics. I'm going to head for a bath and then bed as my legs are so twitchy and I'm just so uncomfortable.

Sunday, 2nd September

I had a bit of respite this morning from doing the breakfasts however David was gone for work by 8am. I still managed to stay in bed for a little while; but when I tried to get organised for my mum coming to visit today I came up against it with Jane. She managed to have a real tantrum and stand-off about wearing something a bit tidier than her normal shabby leggings and t-shirt. We got there in the end but it didn't set the tone too well.

My mum arrived and brought a big lamb casserole for dinner, with raspberries and profiteroles and an iced ginger cake too… Not to mention some lovely freesia flowers and magazines for the kids. We were all spoilt rotten.

It was nice having my mum around and though we all went out after lunch to see a Peter Rabbit exhibition with the kids, I did get some relaxation time later on when they all went to the park. Dinner was amazing. After the kids were in bed my mum wanted to measure my bump… I have no idea what I was before but she remembers that she went up to 46 inches round her waist when she carried me and my sister.

David came home about 8.30pm and we all had a bit of a chat before my Mum left.

I just can't believe we are into September and I'm about to have another baby!

Right, bed before I think about it too much.

Monday, 3rd September

David was up at the crack of dawn at 5am and the kids seemed to be a bit rumbled by it and were up not too long after 6am. Jane had had a bed wetting accident during the night so the day started with washings going on and a shower for Jane.

Once at school, I decided Robbie and I were just going to be staying home this morning. He's still loaded with the cold so not up to his swimming lesson. Well by about 10am this morning I noticed some blood spotting when I went to the toilet. Then by 12.30pm I passed my show and this really got me thinking that I wasn't mistaken about earlier.

I dropped Robbie off at nursery and came home and got right into all the cleaning. I haven't really had much in the way of contractions, just a sore back all day. My neighbour picked up Jane from school and then I went round to get her about 3.30pm. I told her about earlier and she was super excited but I don't want to get my hopes up since I spoke to a midwife on the phone, and she said it might be a sign that labour isn't far away or I could go on like this for another week or so.

I didn't have a great evening with Jane – she got really cheeky after her dinner and started to have a tantrum about not having butter on pancake she was sharing with Robbie! She then started to shout that she hated me and this was the final straw. She was sent to her room for the rest of the night. She was deeply sorry but there was no way I was going to manoeuvre on my decision. It was all cuddles and love by the time we read our stories at bedtime.

David and I had fajitas for dinner tonight, just to try and keep whatever is progressing going! David had his first ISO audit today and did well but he is knackered. He was meant to be going to London tomorrow but I've asked him to cancel it just in case things move forward. I wonder what the night is going to bring!

Friday, 7th September

Well I'm writing this now on Friday 7th September and we are now a very overjoyed family of 5. I can't quite believe it yet. I'll try and recount what happened on Monday night and early hours of Tuesday morning, and draw this book to its final pages!

I decided to have a shower before bedtime, just after 10pm and within minutes of coming out of the shower, at around 10.30pm my waters broke, really quite explosively! I've never quite experienced this before and am so, so glad I wasn't out and about when it did happen! After phoning the hospital they wanted me to come in for an assessment to check waters had gone and no blood present. David's mum and dad got over around midnight and I'd started having contraction's but the pain was manageable. We waited till after 1am and then I was getting stronger contractions about five minutes apart when I finally got my assessment. Our baby's heart rate was monitored for half an hour and I just kept going through the contractions. I had been listening to my hypnobirthing CD since arriving at hospital. The midwife examined me just before 2am and I was 2cm dilated and so David was sent home. She told us that if labour didn't progress then I would be brought back in on Wednesday at 12pm to be induced. At that moment, I had another flood of waters. Probably the fear of being induced! It was clear the midwife didn't think I was getting strong contractions and though I was also headed for home I realised my contractions were now three minutes apart and lasting about one minute so I decided to stay, though I wasn't in a labour ward. I didn't have any more examinations as they just left me to it with my headphones on. I sat on the birthing ball again. It must've been about 4am that I felt that it was getting pretty tough with just the breathing; I sent David a text and buzzed for a midwife. She wanted to examine me but there were no gaps in the contractions to examine me and I knew our baby was actually about to crown and arrive. I remember feeling a real sense of sadness that David wasn't going to be there, but I'd left it too late. The midwives hurried me along to the labour room and within four minutes Liam arrived! It was a shame David wasn't there but such a relief to have our healthy boy. David didn't arrive till nearly an hour later as he never got my second text saying "Get here now!" as he'd fell asleep! Liam is doing fine and was a healthy 7lb 5oz at birth. I think the midwives were shocked that I was so quiet as I did manage to avoid pushing and just breathed Liam down. Liam was born at 4.22am and I'm just so relieved he's here and healthy.

I had to stay in the hospital overnight on the 4th as Liam wasn't feeding brilliantly. He was quite mucousy and sicky because of the speed of his delivery. He's doing great now though and my milk was in within two days. Happy times, the kids have been so excited you could scrape them off the ceiling.

So there ends my pregnancy journal and a new chapter of life's challenges begins.

I wrote this for a few personal reasons however as time progressed I realised it might be interesting and useful for others to read during pregnancy. As a health and fitness professional, I'm sure much of what you've read in my account will be surprising. I hope this reassures future mums-to-be that a healthy balanced attitude to nutrition and exercise is more important. Yes, I desperately wanted to be as healthy as I normally am however my body wanted something else. I ate more when I needed to and as time progressed and I didn't have as big an appetite, or when I was less active, my energy requirements dropped a little too.

My three children are healthy; I didn't gain a massive amount of weight and I managed to return to pre-pregnancy weight fairly quickly.